Use and Abuse
of
America's Natural Resources

Use and Abuse
of
America's Natural Resources

Advisory Editor

STUART BRUCHEY
Allan Nevins Professor of American
Economic History, Columbia University

Associate Editor

ELEANOR BRUCHEY

WILD LIFE CONSERVATION
IN THEORY AND PRACTICE

LECTURES DELIVERED BEFORE THE FOREST
SCHOOL OF YALE UNIVERSITY
1914

By

WILLIAM T. HORNADAY, Sc.D.

ARNO PRESS
A NEW YORK TIMES COMPANY
New York • 1972

Reprint Edition 1972 by Arno Press Inc.

Reprinted from a copy in The University of
Illinois Library

Use and Abuse of America's Natural Resources
ISBN for complete set: 0-405-04500-X
See last pages of this volume for titles.

Manufactured in the United States of America

Library of Congress Cataloging in Publication Data

Hornaday, William Temple, 1854-1937.
    Wild life conservation in theory and practice.

    (Use and abuse of America's natural resources)
    Bibliography: p.
    1. Wildlife conservation--United States. I. Title.
II. Series.
[S964.U6H67 1972]   639'.9'0973   72-2843
ISBN 0-405-04510-7

WILD LIFE CONSERVATION IN THEORY
AND PRACTICE

A LESSON IN BIRD PROTECTION

Wild ducks in the Wichita National Bison Range, Oklahoma, four years after absolute protection from shooting was established.

WILD LIFE CONSERVATION IN THEORY AND PRACTICE

LECTURES DELIVERED BEFORE THE FOREST
SCHOOL OF YALE UNIVERSITY

1914

By

WILLIAM T. HORNADAY, Sc.D.

*Author of "The American Natural History,"
"Our Vanishing Wild Life," etc.;
Ex-President of the Ameri-
can Bison Society*

WITH A CHAPTER ON

PRIVATE GAME PRESERVES

By FREDERIC C. WALCOTT

NEW HAVEN: YALE UNIVERSITY PRESS
LONDON: HUMPHREY MILFORD
OXFORD UNIVERSITY PRESS
MDCCCCXIV

PREFACE

If it is worth while to preserve the wild life of our country, and of the world at large, then it is the duty of the university educators of America to take up their share of the white man's burden. The training of a grand army of embryologists and morphologists is all very well; but what about saving from annihilation the species that our zoölogists are studying? Which is the more important: the saving of the pinnated grouse from extermination, or studying the embryology of a clutch of grouse eggs?

What is needed—and now demanded—of professors and teachers in all our universities, colleges, normal schools and high schools is vigorous and persistent teaching of the ways and means that can successfully be employed in the wholesale manufacture of public sentiment in behalf of the rational and effective protection of wild life.

Thus far the educators of this country as a class and a mass have not done a hundredth part of their duty toward the wild life of the United States and Alaska. Let him who doubts this very sweeping statement ask the next young university or college graduate that he meets how much he has learned in his university about the practical business of pro-

tecting wild life. Let every graduate ask himself
how much he has learned in the classroom of this
highly important branch of zoölogical work.

The course of lectures now published in this
volume represents the awakening of Yale University, through the efforts of Professor James W.
Toumey, Dean of the Forestry School. The
publication of this volume by the University Press
may well be accepted as a contribution to a cause.
It is hoped by those who have made possible this
lecture course and this volume that this presenta-
tion may arouse other educators in our great institutions of learning to take up their shares of the
common burden of conserving our wild life from
the destructive forces that so long have been bearing very heavily upon it. It is not right that this
enormous task should be left to a few toilers—
and fighters—merely because they have, as a matter
of conscience, dedicated themselves to this work.

W. T. H.

University Heights,
    New York City, August 15, 1914.

CONTENTS

FREDERIC C. WALCOTT

LIST OF ILLUSTRATIONS

CHAPTER VI.

CHAPTER I

THE EXTINCTION AND PRESERVATION OF VALUABLE WILD LIFE

The industrial development of the United States has wrought so many sweeping changes from conditions of the past that the American people now are fairly compelled to adjust their minds in conformity with the new conditions. Forty years ago, the preservation of wild life was regarded chiefly as a sentimental cause, of practical interest to sportsmen only. To-day, that cause is not only acutely sentimental, but it has also become intensely practical to millions of American producers and consumers. To-day it affects the lumber-pile, the market-basket and the dinner-pail, and is of such practical importance that it demands the attention of the public at large. A few months ago, on the floor of the United States Senate, Senator Gallinger declared that it is worthy of the serious attention of every man in public life. It is because of our former destructiveness that we now feel the lash of necessity, and are compelled to conserve, whether we will or not.

We will endeavor to present a general view of the present status of the wild life of North America, its practical value to us, and our duty toward it. The time has arrived for the consideration of a number of important practical questions. The amount of exact zoölogical knowledge that has been accumulated in our libraries and museums is enormous. A vast amount of that knowledge is as yet undigested, and much of it seems useless. The academic cabinet naturalist has his place in nature, but the need of the hour is for the economic zoölogist, who can help the producer of crops and the consumer of products to combat the insect world and reduce the appalling cost of living. On this point I feel so strongly that perhaps I am in danger of becoming tiresomely practical; but those who look most deeply into our annual losses in cereal crops, fruit, forests and timber will appreciate my point of view.

We will endeavor to avoid the discussion of academic questions, because the business of conservation is replete with urgent practical demands. It is my desire to offer to the Yale Forest School a foundation on which may be erected a structure of useful knowledge pertaining to the extermination and preservation of the wild life of North America.

To-day it is the way of the world to expect the man who has been educated in a great university to be an encyclopædia of information, and a very present help in time of trouble. Especially is this the case in matters pertaining to conservation. *Noblesse oblige!* The graduates of the forestry schools of the United States will be appealed to, not only for information regarding reforestation, and the insects so destructive to trees, but they will also be called upon to say which species of hawks and owls should be killed, and why; whether all skunks have hydrophobia, and how the gray wolf population may really be reduced. Even yet, wherever large forests remain, there will some remnants of our former abundance of wild life be found. This being the case, it is easily concluded that the men who have to deal with our forests should entertain toward birds, mammals, reptiles and fishes a degree of interest and sympathy that will be manifested in practical protection. We hold that toward our remnant of wild life, every forest ranger, every teacher of forestry and every intelligent American in general, has a solemn duty which no conscientious man can evade.

The Balance of Animate Nature is a subject so well understood by every thoughtful student that it is unnecessary to dwell upon it in detail. To the field naturalist, and the explorer who visits unspoiled lands, it is a subject full of entertainment and delight. In our boyhood days, that is to say about forty years ago, when birds were abundant all over the United States, not even excepting the arboreal deserts, the birds devoured the noxious insects, the hawks and owls devoured the undesired increase of wild rats and mice, and the owls, foxes and lynxes reduced the surplus rabbits. Any undesirable increment in wild life was promptly eaten by its natural enemies; and predatory man, both tame and wild, kept down what might otherwise have been a surplus of bears, foxes, lynxes and other carnivorous animals by trapping them for their fur.

Forty years ago, the spraying of fruit-trees and shade-trees was almost unknown. The only insect enemies of the western farmer and fruit-grower were the grasshopper, tent-caterpillar, the potato-beetle, and at long intervals, the chinch-bug of the wheat-fields. Even after the advent of the Colorado potato-beetle, their black and yellow stripes were so attractive to the rose-breasted grosbeaks that in many localities there were not enough of the beetles to supply the popular demand.

To-day, the farmers, fruit-growers and foresters of the United States are engaged in a hand-to-hand struggle with great armies of destroying insects. It seems as if every bush and tree, and every vegetable, fruit and farm crop has its own special insect plague. Between $7,000,000 and $8,000,000 are expended annually, and in one sense utterly lost, in spraying-machines, poison solutions and labor in fighting insect pests.

For forty years we have been, as a people, criminally destructive of valuable wild life. Now we are paying for the follies of the past. The most foolish of all men is he who needlessly quarrels with a good friend or destroys a valuable ally. Our treatment of our feathered friends, right down to the present hour, is a painful subject; but we must face our own public record and answer to the charges against us.

Whenever man upsets the balance of nature, that moment he begins, in one form or another, to suffer for it and to pay. When the foolish farmers of Pennsylvania demanded and received at Harrisburg a law placing bounties on the heads of slaughtered hawks and owls, by the end of two years those farmers found their fields so overrun by wild rats and mice that they clamored for the quick repeal of the bounty law. Through their losses they learned to appreciate the value of certain hawks and owls as destroyers of noxious rodents.

In 1908, we mentioned the fact that during the previous ten years the woodpeckers of the New York Zoölogical Park had decreased about 90 per cent. In 1912, we noted with sorrow the appearance of the terrible hickory-bark borer, and since that time fully 50 per cent of our hickory trees have been destroyed by that pest. Possibly these two facts are unrelated; but to me their coincidence has a sinister aspect.

It is unfortunate that while so many observations have been made on the anatomy and classification of our wild creatures, more attention has not been paid to their habits and interrelations. The manner in which the lives and habits of our wild allies and foes dovetail together is too little known, and needs to be more seriously studied. It is well that the entomologists are doing their utmost to find parasitic insects that may prey upon the insect species that are so destructive to forests and to crops.

The appalling destruction of wild life that for forty years we have been witnessing on every hand is chargeable to greed, slothfulness and ignorance. The same low order of intelligence that denuded China of her forests, and turned her hillsides into gullied barrenness, has swept away fully 95 per cent of the birds and mammals of America that were most useful to man. Had the game-birds and game-quadrupeds of the United States been properly and conscientiously conserved from the beginning until now, the wild buffalo, elk, deer, turkey, grouse of various species, ducks and geese would to-day be yielding to us each year $10,000,-000 worth of good food that had cost only half a million dollars for warden services to manage it and protect it from unlawful killing.

The destruction and preservation of our wild life has now progressed so far that we can view the future with the lamp of experience. With the past spread out before us like a map, we can see when and wherein we have erred, and we can also measure the practical results of some of our own toil in the field of wild-life conservation. We now are able, with the aid of a little logic, to draw a few conclusions so correct that they are as firmly fixed as the foundations of the Rocky Mountains. Regarding scores of matters that once were questions, and therefore debatable, we now can say that we *know!* It is on the use that we make of our knowledge of existing facts that the future of the wild life of America now depends.

Owing to the sweeping changes that have come upon our wild life during the last twenty years, the young student of to-day needs to be told something of the wild life of the past.

Concerning the former abundance of animal life, a knowledge of the past always gives hope for the future. One of the great natural wonders of the continent of North America, as it came to man from the hand of Nature, was the marvelous variety and abundance of its wild life. *Abundance* is the only word with which to describe the original supply of animal life that stocked our country only a short half century ago. Throughout every state, on every shore-line, in all the millions of fresh-water lakes, ponds and rivers, on every mountain range, in every forest,—aye, even in every desert,—the wild flocks and herds held sway. It was impossible to go beyond the haunts of civilized man and escape them.

The value of the wild life of North America is a subject by itself, which gradually will be developed. In order to become successful conservers of the remnant of that wild life, it is indispensable that we should know in brief the sad story of its past. Patrick Henry spoke wisely when he said,

"I know no way of judging the future but by the past." To-day the question is, Shall we sensibly apply the lessons of the past to the problems of to-day?

It is natural for man to believe that the resources of nature are inexhaustible. The wish is father to the thought. The theory is comforting, because it helps to salve the conscience of the man who commits high crimes against wild beasts, and birds and forests.

In the days of buffalo abundance, the Cree Indians firmly believed that the buffalo herds issued from a great cavern in the earth, and that the supply was quite inexhaustible. The greedy and merciless white buffalo-hunter was so busy with slaughter that he never troubled himself to think about the source of the buffalo supply, or its probable continuance. He said, over and over, "There will always be plenty of buffalo!"

And yet, four years of slaughter, in the early seventies, wiped out the millions of the great southern bison herd; and just ten years later another four years of hide-hunting exterminated the northern herd. Such was the fate of the most numerous, the most conspicuous and most valuable land animal of North America, and the one whose millions were rivaled only by those of the barren-ground caribou.

It is desirable and necessary that every person living should know that systematic slaughter will exterminate the most populous wild species on earth, and accomplish that result in a very few years. Let it be remembered for all time that *no wild species of mammal or bird can withstand systematic slaughter for commercial purposes.*

This applies to all wild mammals that are killed for their skins or their oil, all birds that are killed for their plumage or their flesh, and all game-fishes that are taken for sale. The ocean-going food-fishes withstand the attacks of commerce more successfully than any of the species of wild life that inhabit the land or the small bodies of water.

As a foundation for an exact understanding of the status of wild life in North America, it is necessary to know what man has accomplished, up to date, in the extermination of species. Through the history of the past we can judge clearly and accurately what man can do in the future, both in exterminating and in preserving the remnant. There are occasions when a refusal to heed the lessons of the past becomes a crime. If it is a crime to steal $25, what shall we say of the extermination of a valuable vertebrate species?

The wanton killing of the humblest individual member of the human race, even a man whose vocabulary is limited to two hundred words, is murder, punishable by the severest of all penalties. We hold that there are circumstances under which the killing of a fine wild animal may be so wanton, so revolting and so utterly reprehensible that it may justly be classed as murder. The killing of an American bison for a tongue to sell for fifty cents; the killing of a fine bull elk for a pair of misshapen and ugly teeth worth a dollar; the killing of a walrus "for fun" from the deck of a swiftly moving steamer; the killing of a brown pelican merely to see it fall,—all these are crimes, and should be classed in the annals of crime as murder.

The murder of a wild-animal species consists in taking from it that which man with all his cunning never can give back,—its God-given place in the ranks of living things. Where is man's boasted intelligence, or his sense of proportion, that every man does not see the monstrous moral obliquity involved in the destruction of a species?

Man, the greedy and wasteful spendthrift that he is, has not created even the humblest of the species of mammals, birds and fishes that adorn and enrich this earth. With all his wisdom, and with all his resources, man has not evolved and placed here so much as a ground-squirrel, a sparrow or a clam. It is true that he has juggled with the wild horse and sheep, the goats and the swine, and produced some hardy breeds that can withstand his abuse without going down before it; but as for *species,* man has not yet created and placed in the fauna of this world so much as a protozoan.

As it is with other forms of murder, there are several degrees in wild-life extermination, each of which should be understood.

Local extinction means the complete blotting out of a species over certain specified areas, while the species may exist elsewhere. Thus, in the state of Ohio, the bison, elk, white-tailed deer, puma, black bear, gray wolf, lynx, otter, beaver, wild pigeon, wild turkey, pinnated grouse, pileated woodpecker and Carolina parrakeet all are locally extinct. Throughout fully nine-tenths of its entire former range, the elk has been locally exterminated.

The practical extinction of a species means the destruction of its members to an extent so widespread and so thorough that the species disappears from view, and no living specimens can be found by seeking them. In the United States this is to-day the status of the whooping crane, upland plover, wolverine, California grizzly bear and other species. If any individuals of any of these species are living, they will be found only by accident.

The extermination of a species in a wild state of course means that no individuals of that species are living anywhere save in captivity. This is the case with David's deer of Manchuria, and the passenger pigeon and Carolina parrakeet of North America.

The absolute extermination of a species means that not one individual of it remains alive. Judgment to this effect is based upon the lapse of time since the last individual was seen or killed. When five years have passed without a living "record" of a wild specimen, it is time to place that species in the class of the totally extinct.

To-day the results of man's efforts to exterminate all the most valuable vertebrate life of the North American continent reveal various stages of progress. Eleven species have been totally exterminated in their wild state, and of those all save two, the parrakeet and passenger pigeon, are wholly extinct. The list is as follows:

> Great auk,
> Labrador duck,
> Pallas cormorant,
> Passenger pigeon,
> Eskimo curlew,
> Carolina parrakeet,
> Cuban tricolor macaw,
> Gosse's macaw,
> Yellow-winged green parrot,
> Purple Guadaloupe macaw.

All the above became totally extinct in a wild state between 1840 and 1910.

One other species, the heath-hen or eastern pinnated grouse, the counterpart of the western prairie-chicken, has escaped total extinction only by a very narrow margin. It is so thoroughly extinct locally that to-day it exists only in one locality, on Martha's Vineyard, in eastern Massachusetts, where about two hundred birds are maintained under rigid protection.

The history of the heath-hen teaches a practical lesson that should be of great value to the grouse and other game-birds of to-day, if the men of to-day only will heed it. It is a lesson on the folly of *waiting too long before giving permanent protection!* This bird formerly inhabited Massachusetts, Rhode Island, Connecticut, New York, New Jersey and Pennsylvania. It was the first American game-bird to be brought to the point of extermination by sportsmen.

When its numbers were alarmingly depleted, and attention was strongly called to its impending fate, in the hope of restoring it New York, New Jersey and Massachusetts bestirred themselves, and enacted for the heath-hen protective laws giving it close seasons of five years. At the end of that period, it was found that the species had not perceptibly recovered; so New Jersey and New York gave it close seasons of ten years.

But it was too late! The unfortunate heath-hen completely disappeared, everywhere save on Martha's Vineyard.

The logical conclusion of this episode in extermination is of very great importance to the sportsmen of to-day who heedlessly go on shooting vanishing species of birds, in the belief that such species can at any time be saved and brought back by the application of long-close-season laws. In some cases, the ten-year close season possibly can bring back the candidates for oblivion; and it is well for us that this is true. With every vanishing bird species, however, very soon a point is reached

beyond which it can not recover and come back.
When birds are few and widely scattered, their
natural enemies easily prevent their increase; and
from that point the tendency is downward, until
extinction is reached.

In 1913, after persistent entreaties and far too
long delay, the state of New York accorded her
miserable remnant of quail a five-year close season.
Now the question is, Has the species reached so
low a condition that its natural enemies and winter's
severities will be able to prevent its recovery, as
happened with the heath-hen? The friends of the
quail hope that the relief from persecution has not
come too late; but it is extremely probable that in
many localities of New York the much-beloved
and exceedingly beneficial bob-white is extinct
forever.

Let the college men of America carry this mes-
sage to every American sportsman and lawmaker
throughout the length and breadth of the land.
Say to them: "Beware! A point can be reached
by a vanishing species beyond which it can not
recover, and long close seasons are in vain. Do
not delay until that fatal point has been passed.
Restocking barren covers by importing quail is a
delusion and a snare. The Hungarian partridge
is a failure, and it can not be made to take the place
of our own grouse and quail. Give every en-
dangered species a five-year close season. Do it at

once; and when that limit has expired, give it another."

Wherever killable wild life is found, [greed and ignorance are quite as deadly as shot-guns.] At this moment, the gunners and sportsmen of Nebraska, Oklahoma, Iowa and Minnesota diligently and even joyously exercise the right that their state lawmakers still foolishly extend them to hunt and kill the pinnated grouse. In those states the man-with-a-gun is deaf to the appeal to reason, blind to the lessons of history. If the law continues its per-mission, those gunners very soon will shoot down the last pinnated grouse. Yes; very earnest efforts *have* been made to awaken those sodden people, but thus far in vain. In view of the army of gunners, the uncountable thousands of guns, the dogs, wagons, automobiles, tents and other munitions of war that annually take the field against the prairie-chicken remnant, every observer is compelled to believe that without a quick and sweeping reform, the end of the species is in sight.

At the same time other species, elsewhere, are similarly threatened. Consider the sage-grouse and the sharp-tailed grouse of the northwestern quarter of our great plains; the wild turkey in half a dozen states; the quail in a dozen states; the shore-birds of every species; the sandhill and whooping cranes; the swan; the ptarmigan; the mule deer in several states; the mountain sheep in Wyoming, Montana, Idaho and Washington.

The lists of species of birds and mammals that already have been locally exterminated in the various states of our country make in the aggregate an appalling showing. We do not need to grieve over the species that because of their size and habits were foredoomed to disappear before the thick settlements and fierce progress of civilization; but we are unreconciled to the needless extinction of species that could and would have survived had they been conserved on a sensible basis, and that could and would have yielded an annual increase of great value to man.

At this moment, in addition to the eleven species of birds already totally exterminated on our continent, there are at least twenty-five others that are prominent candidates for oblivion. Several of these have already been mentioned. The groups that are in greatest peril are the shore-birds (sixty species) and the grouse. Fortunately, all of the former save six species recently (October 1, 1913) have come under the protection of the federal migratory bird law. Unfortunately, however, none of the members of the grouse family are so protected, and it is among them that serious fatalities are impending.

Prior to October 1, 1913, there was another phase of bird destruction that gave the conservators of wild life very great concern. It was the destruction of insectivorous birds of many species by the Italians of the North and the negroes of the South, and in some localities by white men calling themselves sportsmen but lacking anything even remotely resembling a code of ethics in shooting.

Although in general it is our duty to let bygones be bygones, and not rake up the disagreeable embers of the past, we are not yet so far on the road to reform that we need ignore the things of yesterday. The martins, swallows, nighthawks, robins and bobolinks that have been shot in the South by sportsmen as "game" and for "food," and the doves that have been slaughtered all the way from the Carolinas to California, still cry out for protection for the remnant.

A little later we will consider more fully the relations of birds and mammals to agriculture, horticulture and forestry. This subject is of vast importance to our country, and in view of the extent to which it already is understood by the most intelligent of our American farmers, it is strange that the logic of the situation has not produced more thorough and universal protection for the farmers' feathered friends and allies.

In order to lay a foundation for a comprehensive knowledge of the subject before us, it is imperatively necessary that the forces operating for the extermination of wild life should be thoroughly known.

To-day this country of ours is the theater of a remarkable struggle between the great forces of destruction and the small forces of protection and preservation. In every township throughout the whole United States the destroyers of wild life either are active in slaughter or are ready to become active the moment they are left free to do so. Every beast, bird, fish and creeping thing has its human enemy. Americans are notoriously enterprising, restless and prone to venture. It is that restless activity and indomitable nervous energy that is manfully attempting "dry-farming" in the West, desert-farming in the Southwest, and the drainage of the Florida Everglades. Often the joy of the conquest of nature outruns the love of cash returns. Apply that spirit to forests, and it quickly becomes devastation. Apply it to wild life, and it quickly becomes extermination.

Our conquering and pulverizing national spirit is a curse to all our wild life. The native of India permits the black buck, the sand grouse and the saras crane to roam over his fields unmolested for two thousand years. The American, and the Englishman also, at once proceeds to shoot all of that wild life that he can approach within range. In America, the national spirit may truthfully be expressed in the cry of the crazed Malay: *"Amok! Amok!"* "Kill! Kill!" This is why the conservation of valuable wild life is in our country a fearfully difficult task, from which most people shrink and seek something either more pleasant or personally profitable.

It may be accepted as absolutely certain that if

the forces that now protect wild life were withdrawn from the field, and the destroyers were permitted to go their way unchecked, in ten years' time the whole United States would be as barren of valuable and desirable wild life as is Italy to-day. Imagine the carnival of slaughter that would ensue!

Although the remnant of game birds and quadrupeds now alive in the United States represents only about 2 per cent of the stock that existed here only fifty years ago, that remnant is sufficient to cause the sale each year, in this country, of nearly half a million shot-guns, and about 500,000,000 cartridges. We are not taking into this account the additional 400,000,000 cartridges that are used annually in trap-shooting.

The army of destruction that annually takes the field against wild life, openly and according to law, contains at least 2,642,194 men and boys. Through a little investigation we found in 1911 that twenty-seven of our states issued hunting licenses, and that the total number actually issued for that year was 1,486,228, or an average of 55,046 for each state.[1]

The twenty-one states not issuing hunting licenses, or not reporting, undoubtedly sent as many hunters per capita into the field in 1911 as did the other states. Computed fairly on existing averages, those twenty-one states were undoubtedly

[1] In 1912, when Pennsylvania enacted a license law covering the hunting privilege, it was estimated that 200,000 hunting licenses would be issued each year. In 1913 the actual number proved to be nearly 300,000!

responsible for 1,155,966 men and boys hunting in 1911 according to law, making up the grand total of more than 2,600,000 previously mentioned.

To this vast body we must add another grand army of gunners, believed to be equally large, hunting contrary to law and without licenses, and killing wild creatures, game and non-game, in season and out of season, to an extent of slaughter fully as great as that perpetrated by the licensed hunters.

Now for an illustration of the practical effect of our grotesque and absurd national system of game protection.

The state of Utah is, with the exception of its irrigated lands, a desert state. Its stock of game, excepting the migratory ducks of Great Salt Lake, is at a very low point. The population of the state is only 373,351, but in 1911 that state sent an army of 27,800 well-armed men into the field against her pitiful remnant of game birds and quadrupeds. And this sort of thing the people of America call "game protection"!

In addition to the hunters themselves who annually take the field, they are assisted by thousands of expert guides, thousands of well-trained dogs, thousands of horses, thousands of wagons and automobiles, and hundreds of thousands of tents. Each big-game hunter provides himself with an experienced local guide who knows the haunts and habits of the game, the best feeding-grounds, the best trails, and everything else that will aid the hunter in taking the game at the utmost disadvantage and destroying it most thoroughly. The big-game rifles are of the highest power, the longest range and the greatest rapidity of fire that modern inventive genius and mechanical skill can produce.

Every appliance and assistance that money can buy, the modern sportsman and gunner diligently secures to help him in destroying his chosen game. The deadliness of the automobile in hunting is already so well recognized that North Dakota has enacted a law forbidding its use against the game of that state. The superior deadliness of the automatic and pump shot-guns is thoroughly and widely acknowledged by the popularity of those weapons with the men who wish to kill all that the law allows. Look carefully at the published photographs of game-hogs and their masses of slaughtered ducks, geese, quail and other birds, and in about nine out of every ten of them you will find the automatic shot-gun or the pump-gun, or both.

The grand army of men and boys who hunt according to law assails the game during the annual open season. The poachers and the resident hunters kill it all the year round, and rarely are any of them caught and convicted. I am convinced that this class of killers is doing far more toward the extinction of species than is done by sportsmen. It is the market-gunner, however, who is most deadly of all. He works early and late, at least six days a week, and the game he seeks knows no

respite. His skill in shooting is fatal to the game,
and wherever market-hunting is permitted, its final
result is the extermination of the game in the
locality affected.

During its breeding season the game is beset by
its natural enemies—foxes, cats, hawks, owls,
wolves, lynxes and other predatory species; and to
this must be added the cold and starvation of extra-
severe winters.

The bag limits, on which vast reliance has been
placed to preserve our game from extinction, are a
fraud, a *delusion* and a *snare!* The few local
exceptions only prove the generality of the rule.
In every state, without one single exception, the
bag limits are far too high, and the laws are of
deadly liberality. I think that in most states the
bag-limit laws on birds are an absolute dead letter.
Fancy ninety-five wardens in the state of New York
enforcing the bag-limit laws on 150,000 licensed
gunners! In British East Africa, for a license cost-
ing $250, you receive a lawful right to kill three
hundred head of big game, representing forty-four
species,—almost enough to load a ship.

From 1885 to 1900, the agents of the millinery
trade wrought great destruction among the birds of
North America. In the beginning of the craze for
stuffed birds and wild birds' plumage on women's
hats, all kinds of bright-colored song-birds, terns,
gulls, herons, egrets, spoonbills, ibises and the
flamingo were used. The small birds were mounted

entire, and the larger species were used piecemeal.
The slaughter for millinery purposes called forth,
as the special champion of birds, the Audubon
Societies, state and national. Their first work consisted in prohibiting the use of song-birds, and in
stopping the killing of gulls and terns. The Audubon people stepped in at a time when a furious and
bloody general slaughter of our gulls and terns
was in progress, and they literally brought back to
us those interesting and pleasing species. But for
their efforts, there would to-day be only the merest
trace of the long-winged swimmers along our
Atlantic coast.

In the South, no power proved sufficient to save
the unfortunate egrets and herons, the ibises, spoonbills and flamingo. The flamingo is totally extinct
throughout the United States, and of the other
species, nothing more than sample specimens remain. Of the white egrets, there are about twenty
small colonies, each one protected from the rapa-
cious plume-hunters by Audubon Society wardens
or by the national government.

But the destroyers of wild life have not been permitted to have everything their own way. To-day
their progress is contested by an army of defenders,
which, in the greatest battles that have been fought
in our country, have been completely victorious.
Enough victories have been won to demonstrate the
fact that it is possible to save the remnant of wild
life, and increase it.

The defenders of wild life have accomplished results along the following lines:

1. Seventy per cent of the killing of non-game-birds has been stopped.

2. The killing of game has been restricted to open seasons, which have steadily been made shorter.

3. Long close seasons, usually for five years, have been extended to a very few species threatened with local extinction.

4. The sale of game has been prohibited in seventeen states.

5. They have achieved the complete suppression of the importation of wild birds' plumage for millinery, and the equally complete suppression of the use of native birds as hat ornaments.

6. They have brought about the creation of a really great number of national and state game-preserves and bird refuges.

7. There has been a partial suppression of the use of extra-deadly firearms in killing birds.

8. Finally, the army of defense has secured the enactment of a law placing all our 610 species of migratory birds under the protection of the federal government.

Of all these protective and restrictive measures, the one of greatest importance to the orchards and forests of our country is the law for the federal protection of migratory birds, named in honor of Senator George P. McLean of Connecticut, who introduced and successfully advocated in the Senate the measure that finally was enacted into law. This measure was championed in and through the House of Representatives by Mr. John W. Weeks of Massachusetts, now a senator.

There is one item of history connected with that measure which forcibly illustrates the state of public feeling regarding the birds that are of practical value to trees and crops. All of six years ago, a bill was introduced in Congress for the federal protection of migratory *game-birds*. It was ably championed by its author, Mr. George Shiras, 3d, but in five years it made no progress. Subsequent bills of the same character were introduced by other members of Congress, but so long as they provided for the game-birds only, there was no great public demand for their passage, and they slumbered peacefully in the committees to which they had been referred.

Finally, in 1912, the insectivorous birds were made the leading issue of a great national campaign that was waged in behalf of the amended McLean bill. On that issue the support of the press and the people at large was actively enlisted, and in spite of some doubts regarding its constitutionality, and its possible infringement of the rights of states, the measure passed the Senate without one dissenting vote. Later on it passed the House opposed by only fifteen votes. To insure action upon it, the measure finally was incorporated in the Agricultural Appropriation Bill, and so riding it became a law.

Stated most briefly, the new law provides that the Secretary of Agriculture shall frame regulations for the protection, by the national government, of all the birds of the United States that do not abide continuously in any one locality, but pass from state to state. The regulations first proposed by the Secretary of Agriculture were published three months in advance of their becoming effective and during that period all persons interested were at liberty to be heard upon them, either in objection or in approval. At the end of three months, by a presidential proclamation which was issued on October 1, 1913, the final draft of the regulations became a federal law.

The federal migratory bird law as now in force is the most potent and far-reaching measure ever enacted for the protection of our native birds, and any occurrence that would impair or destroy its usefulness would be a national and continental calamity. Its most important features are the following:

1. It stops all spring shooting of migratory birds.

2. It will stop the slaughter of song-birds, swallows, the migratory woodpeckers and other insectivorous birds.

3. It confers a five-year close season on all save six of our sixty species of shore-birds.

4. It shortens the northern season on water-fowl to about three months—a period quite long enough.

5. It renders the protection of the wood-duck universal.

The federal bill divides the United States into two life-zones, with differences between the two, in the regulations, which now are causing some local irritation; but this state of feeling will subside as soon as the aggrieved ones can be made to understand that *at present* the regulations represent the best wisdom and the best efforts of the Government, pending an actual trial of the principles involved.

As in times past when "the prayers of the church" were invoked in behalf of persons in peril or distress, so do we now need to invoke the sympathy and sustaining influence of the American people at large in behalf of both the federal migratory bird law and the international treaty now being negotiated with Canada for the protection of the migratory birds of the continent. *The law is necessary because of the utter inability of more than one-half of our states to protect their migratory birds by state laws.* For twenty years, at least, fifteen states have sullenly refused to heed the demands made in behalf of the common welfare. The states of Maryland, Virginia, the two Carolinas, Georgia, Arkansas, Texas, Tennessee, Kentucky, and until 1913 California also, have one and all been deplorably remiss in their treatment of bird life, and grossly unfair to the states northward of them. For example, Iowa had most obstinately and selfishly refused to enact a law against spring shooting, even after a great number of other states had done so. Now the federal law has terminated that irritating situation,—as we believe, forever.

A state or a nation can be uncivil, ungentlemanly or mean, just the same as an individual. The new bird law "shines like a good deed in a naughty world," because it puts the screws of compulsion upon a number of mean and greedy states that toward wild life have manifested little sense of honor or of decency. Those who have labored longest in the vineyard of protection rejoice that they have lived to see the day when states like Maryland, the Carolinas and Iowa will be forced to give the migratory birds of the United States and Canada a square deal.

From the very first inception of the idea of a federal law for the benefit of the migratory birds, its friends have feared that it would be attacked by the professional champions of the states' rights fetich, as an infringement on the prerogatives of the so-called "sovereign states." It was particularly feared that on this ancient ground much opposition to the bill would come from the southern states.

To the everlasting credit of all the southern states let it be stated, that up to this hour *no* south-

The Kind of Deer-Hunting That Means Extermination!

Does and Fawns. Montana, 1913.

ern man or body of men has raised this question!
On the contrary, much of the enthusiastic support
of "the McLean bill" and "the Weeks bill" came
from southern protectors of wild life, particularly
from Alabama, Tennessee and Texas. So far as the
southern states are concerned, the old southern
states' rights bogey seems to be dead, and we have
no fear that an attack on the new bird law ever will
be made by southern men.

But how is it in the North?

Time brings many changes, some of them both
startling and absurd. In the Fifth National Conservation Congress, held at Washington in 1913,
the main assault on the principle of federal control
of water-power for the benefit of the people of the
nation at large, was led by the representatives of
northern states, who set up a loud demand for state
control, and state rights!

The state of New York refused to join in that
demand, but later on, the people of that common-
wealth were treated to a surprise all their own. In
reply to an inquiry from the New York State Conservation Commission regarding the status of certain trivial differences between the federal bird law
and the New York state bird laws, Attorney-
General Carmody propounded and published an
official opinion to the effect that the federal migratory bird law is unconstitutional, and therefore void
and of no effect in New York state. Later on, he

announced that he would insist upon the enforcement of his opinion throughout the state.

The only serious effect of the attorney-general's opinion was that its publication in a great many newspapers, with the startling head-line *"Federal Bird Law Declared Unconstitutional,"* gave many timid persons a momentary scare, and an impression that the law really may be unconstitutional.

The champions of the bird law lost not a moment in challenging the soundness of the opinion, and in pointing out that a street-car conductor or a barber can as easily nullify a federal law by pronunciamento as can any state attorney-general. Their claim that the attorney-general's opinion was purely academic, so far as the enforcement of the federal law is concerned, was quickly substantiated by a statement from an assistant attorney-general for the United States, Mr. Kroetel, who informed the people of New York that the migratory bird law is in full force in that state, and its enforcement by the national government will assuredly continue. Although scores of newspapers between Chicago and Boston have commented editorially on this comedy of much ado about nothing, only one has supported the position assumed by our attorney-general, while all the others have severely condemned it. The law is in full force in New York state, and it will be enforced down to the utmost detail, until it is either repealed by Congress, or set aside by the United States Supreme Court,—

neither of which is at all likely ever to occur. At least twenty-five competent lawyers carefully studied the McLean bill before it became a law, and became convinced that what it proposed would be entirely constitutional.

We mention this case in some detail for two reasons. The first is to make it clear that the absurd performance of New York's chief law officer has not even made a dent in the armor of the McLean law, and that the law is everywhere an existing fact, pending action by a federal court of last resort.[1]

The second reason is to point out the fact that the friends and champions of wild life must be constantly *on the alert and ready to fight,* and sometimes must undertake the painful duty of chastising their own friends when those friends go wrong, and attack the cause of protection on academic grounds.

The sale of game has already been mentioned as one of the most powerful agencies employed in the

[1] The first decision on the status of the migratory law was that rendered in South Dakota on April 18, 1914, by Judge J. D. Elliott of the Federal Court, who decided, in the case of A. M. Shaw, that the law is constitutional. Mr. Shaw pleaded guilty, and was fined $100, which was paid.

In the eastern district of Arkansas, at Jonesboro, on May 27, in the United States District Court, the case of the United States against Harvey C. Schauver, for a violation of the federal migratory bird law, was heard by Judge Jacob Trieber, who decided that "the law is unconstitutional." Of course the United States will carry the case up until it finally reaches the United States Supreme Court, where, with extra expedition, a decision may be expected in about eighteen months. The Arkansas decision affects only the eastern district of that state, and elsewhere the law will be strictly enforced.

destruction and extermination of our wild birds. The destruction of game-birds by sportsmen is trifling in comparison with the slaughter by commerce. Quite recently there was published in a sportsmen's magazine the records of individual slaughter that had been made and kept for forty years by a professional market-hunter. Having a liking for bookkeeping, the hunter kept accurate and continuous records. Here are the main items, and the grand total: In a three-months' shoot in Iowa and Minnesota, he killed 6,250 game-birds. In one winter's duck hunting in the South, he killed 4,450 ducks. During his forty years' market-hunting he killed 61,752 ducks, 5,291 prairie-chickens, 8,117 useful *blackbirds,* 5,291 quail, 5,066 snipe and 4,948 plover. His grand total of slaughter was 139,628 game-birds and sundries, representing twenty-nine species, several of them not game and *useful.*

During the past fifteen years, many states have gradually been cleaning house in the matter of the commercial slaughter of their game, and many good half-way laws have been enacted. The original rule was for a state to protect its own game, but to permit the sale of game slaughtered in other states. This essentially selfish basis led to an immense amount of mutual poaching and selling, and the results were most disastrous.

In 1911, the state of New York led the way in a sweeping reform. The legislature enacted the

now famous Bayne law, which absolutely prohibits
the sale in that state of any American wild game,
no matter where killed, and strictly limits the sale
of all foreign game. It does permit the importation and sale of six species of game birds and
mammals that are very commonly killed in Europe
on preserves and sold for food; and it also permits
the sale, under official state tags, of white-tailed
deer, mallard ducks, black ducks and pheasants
that have been bred and reared *in captivity* in New
York, and killed and tagged according to law.

This law had the immediate and visible effect of
stopping fully one-half of the enormous annual
duck and goose slaughter on Currituck Sound,
North Carolina, and it directly benefited each
of the sixteen states in the line of annual flight of
about 150,000 unkilled wild fowl. The action of
New York was immediately followed by similar
action in Massachusetts; after which, in 1913, the
state of California also wheeled into line. The
California law is now being attacked by a petition
for a referendum, and the enemies of wild life
have found 20,000 persons who were unwise enough
to sign against the new law.

At present the principal remaining plague-spots
for the sale of wild game are New Haven, Provi-
dence, Baltimore, Washington, Richmond, Atlanta,
Chicago and Denver.

The most sweeping victory for birds that up to
this date (1914) has been achieved was that which

on October 4, 1913, set over the birds of the world an impenetrable shield for their protection from the feather millinery trade of America.   This was accomplished through a clause in the new tariff bill absolutely prohibiting the importation of any fancy feathers, plumes, skins or quills of wild birds other than the ostriches and domestic fowls, for commercial uses.   Thus was there achieved in this country, after six months of diligent labor, a result for which England throughout six years has striven in vain, but which now is near attainment, through a government measure known as "the Hobhouse bill."   The clause in the new tariff bill, drafted by and championed by the New York Zoölogical Society, gave the women and men of America the first opportunity that ever had been offered them to strike one crushing blow at the feather millinery disgrace.

The opportunity was improved to the utmost, and after the fiercest battle ever waged in the United States Senate over any measure for the protection of wild life, the protection cause completely triumphed.   To-day the ports of the United States and its colonial possessions are absolutely closed to the plumage of wild birds.   As a first result, consider the great quarterly feather sale in London on October 14.   On account of the closing of the American market, more than one-third of all the feathers offered there were unsalable, and had to be withdrawn.   In Berlin, the price of aigrettes has

fallen 20 per cent, and in Paris the milliners fear
that the fashion for aigrettes is as good as dead,
because their best customers can wear them no
more.

The sweeping prohibition that we have enacted
sets the pace for the civilized world. The suppression of the cruel slaughter of the innocents at the
behest of fashion and vanity and commercial greed,
was here treated as a cause involving the honor of
the nation. To-day the people of England, Hol-
land, France and Germany are appealing to their
governments on the same basis. *The honor of
nations* demands the suppression of bird slaughter
for plumage; and assuredly that suppression will
come, and be made general. The crusade affects
at least a hundred species of the most beautiful and
curious birds of the world, the most of them to-day
quite unprotected, so far as the laws of their home
countries are concerned.

In assembling our conclusions, we find that the
first relates to *the state of the public mind.*

During the past fifteen years, the improvement
in that direction has been enormous! To-day, drastic measures can be enacted into law which even ten
years ago would have been deemed visionary,
fanatical and wildly impossible. To-day a million
American people are anxious to atone for their past
follies in the destruction of wild life. To-day, the
man who proposes a great reform, and appeals to
the mass of people who *do not shoot wild life,* soon

finds both sympathy and support. The greater the cause, the greater its chances for success—provided a fair amount of time, labor and money is judiciously expended on the campaign.

With a campaign fund of $5,000,—to be expended chiefly in printer's ink and postage,—we would guarantee to give any state in this union a new code of modern protective laws in eight months' time. The greatest factor in reforming the wild-life situation is *education:* for it is the educated people who educate their *legislators* into the making of better laws and providing means for their enforcement.

At this moment the minds of millions of Americans are, toward wild life, like negatives all ready to receive definite impressions regarding the needs of the hour. And imagine, if you please, what it would mean to the wild life of the nation if every college and university graduate should go forth with a good working knowledge of the wild-life situation, coupled with a fully aroused sense of personal duty toward it. Is it not a very great pity that only a few of our universities pay attention to this subject, and that through a lack of attention the services of what might have been a mighty host of crusaders has been lost!

The men and women of this country who for years have been toiling to save the wild life of the nation have wrought because they have been spurred by a sense of duty; merely this and nothing

more. We of to-day have no right to destroy, or to
permit others to destroy, the *principal* of a wild-
life inheritance that belongs to posterity fully as
much as to ourselves. We hold the wild life of our
glorious land IN TRUST, and it is our duty to protect
it adequately from the spendthrifts who would
foolishly butcher it and destroy it.

Thanks to the fighting that already has been
done, the army of destruction has been routed on
many a field, and its entire line of battle has been
checked. I wish it were in our power to speak to
every American who loves his country and say that
it pays to fight in this cause. In 1912, a band of
teachers, curators and students in the University
of California decided that it was their bounden
duty to put forth a supreme effort to save the wild
birds and mammals of that state from the annihilation that was then in full progress. They addressed themselves to the task before them like
men! They organized an army of defense such as
California never before had seen; and they taught
the sportsmen of California the foundation principles of real campaigning in behalf of wild life.

In the terrific conflict that ensued, in which
nearly every large newspaper in the state was
bitterly arrayed against them, they never wavered
or looked back. Eventually the contest ended in
an almost complete victory for the wild-life cause,
and in a manner that reflected great credit on the
University of California.

The most important conclusion to be drawn from the records of the past is that *it is quite possible* to save the existing remnants of our continental stock of wild life, and also *entirely practicable*. It is a matter of individual effort and campaign-expense money. Five years ago the cause seemed almost hopeless, and many persons predicted that in a few years no large game would remain anywhere in the United States outside of rigidly protected game preserves. But, thanks to the energy and persistence of the men and women on the firing-line, that gloomy expectation has been dissipated. It is now admitted that the extermination of a species is a crime; that the wild life of the nation belongs more to the 97 per cent of people who do not go hunting and do not kill, than to the 3 per cent who do. It has been found that large men prefer to aid large measures, and it costs not much more to enact a great bill into law than it does to promote a small one. It has been demonstrated that millions of people are quite willing to promote the protection of wild life if they are only informed, and told what to do, and reasonably led. The fact that it has been proven possible to secure practical results has encouraged thousands to take hold.

The success and popularity of the national parks and national game-preserves has led to great activities in that particular field of endeavor. The Yellowstone Park, with its herds of bear, mountain sheep, antelope, mule deer, bison and moose, led straight to Glacier Park, the magnificent, with its 1,400 square miles of towering peaks, plunging valleys, glaciers, lakes and forests. As a public reservoir for mountain goats, sheep, grizzly bear, black bear and moose, it is a domain that we can hand down to posterity with the utmost pride. There is reason to believe that it will preserve the mountain goat from extinction in the United States. The magnificent forests of Douglas and Engelmann spruce, white pine, white cedar and fir that fill its valleys and fringe its lakes are a priceless heritage. While we think of it, we are reminded how utterly and hopelessly marred would be that grand mountain fastness if our forbears had wantonly destroyed all that timber, as the men and boys of yesterday and to-day were striving, and are striving, to annihilate all our finest beasts and birds.

No one thanks an ancestor who hands over to him only desolation, ugliness and poverty.

In addition to the Yellowstone and Glacier parks, our group of national parks includes the Mt. Olympus National Monument in the Olympic mountains of Washington, a wild, rugged and little-known region of rough mountains and heavy timber, inhabited by about 1,200 elk. In the arid regions, the Grand Canyon National Park has been created, to include 101 miles of the awful meanderings of the mighty chasm, its northern and western side literally reeking with pumas and wolves that subsist on mule deer and mountain sheep. There are several smaller national parks, such as Sequoia,—for the big redwood trees,— Yosemite, General Grant and Crater Lake.

Of great importance to the American bison are the four national bison ranges that have been created especially for the perpetuation of that species. Two of these have been stocked by the New York Zoölogical Society and one by the American Bison Society. The four are located as follows: in the Wichita Mountains, southwestern Oklahoma; in the southern end of the old Flathead Indian reservation near Ravalli, Montana; at Wind Cave, in the southern terminus of the Black Hills, South Dakota; and the old Fort Niobrara Military Reservation, in Nebraska.

In the national parks and national game-preserves no hunting is allowed; and these are indeed wild-life preserves. In the vast stretches of the national forests that plentifully blotch with green the map of the western third of the United States, hunting *is* allowed in accordance with the state laws; and beyond all possibility of serious question, the killable wild life is rapidly vanishing from those areas. There is no reason to believe that anywhere in North America where hunting is allowed, any species of big game except wolves are breeding more rapidly than they are being killed. *Every national forest should be made a hard and fast national game-preserve,* in which no hunting for

sport ever should be permitted. Of course the
noxious wild animals must be killed; but that is
another story.

Let me offer one painful illustration of the folly
of leaving to the states the preservation of their
game, as the sport of politics and favoritism, when
it is possible for the nation at large to preserve it.
At this moment the states of Wyoming, Montana
and Idaho actually permit by law the hunting and
killing of their pitiful remnants of mountain sheep.
Their laws provide for the killing of rams only,
and are supposed to protect the females for breeding purposes. But do they really preserve the
breeding female sheep? Emphatically they do not.
*Wherever sheep or goats are killed, the females
disappear fully as rapidly as the males!* Is it not
strange that none of those states have taken note
of this? The result is steady and sure extermination! Wyoming has to-day hardly more than one
hundred wild sheep on her hunting-grounds, and
the rapacity and determination with which those
sheep are hunted by gentlemen sportsmen and their
hired guides has an aspect that is positively fiendish.

The moment the national forests become national
game-preserves, from that moment those mountain
sheep are assured of real protection.

The laws of the western and Pacific coast states
have been dictated chiefly by the sportsmen—the
men who kill. They insist upon open seasons, as
long as any killable game remains. The pressure

of the organized sportsmen on the western state legislator is too great for the best interests of the wild life. What shall be done?

A great step remains to be taken. Ten years ago, when the national forest idea was fighting for its life in Congress, even the President did not dare to mention above a whisper the logical conclusion of the western big-game situation, which is this:

In the near future, Congressional legislation must be enacted which will make of every national forest a national game-preserve, in which no hunting for sport is permitted.

Whenever such a demand is formally launched, a roar of disapproval and protest will arise from the men of the West who now hunt in the national forests, and are bent on maintaining their killing privileges. As was the case with the Bayne bill against the sale of game, the cry will be raised: "Too drastic! Too sweeping! Revolutionary! It means prohibition of hunting," etc. But we have heard all this many times before. The thing to do, all over the world, is to save the wild life even though slaughtering privileges are cut off in the doing of it.

Regarding their game, the western mountain states have well-nigh sinned away their days of grace. Let them alone a little longer, and they will be as barren of all game as the Colorado desert. In legal parlance, they have slept on their rights,—

their state rights to preserve their game in fact as well as in name.

A little later, when Congress has recovered from the weariness of the conflict over feather millinery, we will ask for the legislation that will be necessary to turn each and every national forest-reserve into a haven of refuge and a sanctuary inviolate for the harassed wild birds and mammals that *must* find in them shelter and life, or perish.

When the time comes for us to undertake that task, we will call upon the men of Yale, both within these walls and without them, to make that task their own. If it were only possible to induce American college men at large to give active aid in that mighty struggle, a victory would positively be assured. The cause will loom so large that it should attract large men and commend itself to every statesman in Congress.

Look at a map showing the national forest-reserves. Those reserves belong to the people of the nation at large—partly to you and to me. Shall we not exercise our lawful right to stop game slaughter within their borders? Think what such a step would mean to the wild life of the western third of our country and to posterity,—to both of which we owe duties that we can not *with honor* neglect or evade.

CHAPTER II

THE ECONOMIC VALUE OF OUR BIRDS

After twenty years of more or less constant educational work and legislative warfare, some of the birds of our country, that make war on the insect world, and protect our crops and forests, have at last come to their own. The passage of the McLean-Weeks federal migratory bird bill, in May, 1913, into the federal migratory bird law, was the crowning effort of a long and arduous series of campaigns! The bill was driven through both houses of Congress by a tornado of popular demand. For five years or longer, the Shiras bill for the federal protection of migratory *game*-birds had slumbered in the pigeon-holes of the committees to which it had been referred, for the simple reason that the public at large was not deeply interested in the federal protection of birds that were destined only to be slaughtered by all kinds of gunners, and especially market-gunners.

The amending of the McLean bill, by a provision for the protection of the *insectivorous* birds generally, had the immediate effect of galvanizing the whole measure into life. The press of the country, the granges, the Audubonists, the sportsmen and the friends of birds at large filed such insistent and persistent demands for the law that Congress was amazed; and it is a well-known fact that several senators who doubted the constitutionality of the McLean bill purposely refrained from voting against it because of the strength of the popular demand for the law.

And well may the producers and consumers of food and timber desire the protection of the birds that help to protect the crops and the trees at large from the insect hordes that are ever present to destroy root, branch, leaf, flower and fruit. It is indeed high time for the forester and the lumberman to become practical bird protectionists, and devote both time and effort to the making of laws, and the enforcement of laws, for the thorough protection of all birds that consume the insect enemies of trees. I believe it is no exaggeration to estimate that more trees are annually destroyed in the United States by insects than are destroyed by fire; and yet much more is said about the protection of forests from fires than from insects. Some of the far western states, particularly Washington and Oregon, have been flooded with admirable fire-alarm circulars and posters; but has any state lumbermen's association, or any organization of forest protectors, ever made a whirlwind campaign for the better protection of forests from insects?

Fires are spectacular and tragic, and it is natural that they should fix public attention far more than the bark-beetles, wood-borers and leaf-destroyers that work so silently and yet so fatally. The fire-watchers of the great forest regions of the far West are ceaselessly diligent in watching for smoke from peak summit and lofty tower, and telephoning the news of every fire observed; but no one is able to exercise any such protective vigilance against the ravages of insects. In the general slaughter of wild life, the most valuable of tree-protecting birds have been rapidly fading away. We first note their disappearance by the fact that they are much less numerous than formerly, and finally are becoming rare; and we know that they are shot and eaten by the northern Italian and the southern negro.

For many reasons, it seems both desirable and necessary that every friend and protector of bird life should be armed with precise information regarding the economic value of our birds. In protective warfare, such facts are continually called for, particularly by newspaper reporters and editors, magazine writers, members of law-making bodies, and even judges on the bench who are friendly and anxious to help. The amount of exact information that must each year be furnished for practical use regarding the value of our insectivorous birds is enormous, and the demand for such information is certain to be continuous.

Let no friend of the birds be deceived into the belief that because the federal migratory bird law is

now on the national statute books, the birds necessarily are safe, without further campaigning. That
is far from being the case. The struggle for the
saving and bringing back of the birds is our new
"irrepressible conflict." Let us look the situation
squarely in the eyes, and prepare ourselves for what
is inevitable.

*Just so long as any wild birds live there will be
deadly enemies seeking to destroy them; and it is
our bounden duty to be constantly on the alert, and
ready to repel the attack of every foe.* Just so
long as repressive protective laws remain upon our
statute books will the enemies of wild life strive to
repeal or nullify them.

Let us briefly review the investigations and the
facts that have demonstrated the commercial and
industrial value of our wild birds. Naturally,
foresters will be interested in hearing first of the
birds that benefit the trees of our country.

Thousands of species of insects feed upon and
shelter in the trees of the street, the park, the
orchard and the forest. It is no exaggeration to
assert that every tree has its insect enemies. The
chief points of attack are the bark and the leaves;
but the wood also is attacked by many destructive
borers. To one who loves trees, who has planted
hundreds with his own hands and caused the planting of thousands more, there are times when the
work of the insect pests become fairly heartbreak-
ing. The awful chestnut blight, which is due to a

fungus, not an insect, was first discovered in the northeastern states in the New York Zoölogical Park, by its chief forester, and it was then and there that a fierce battle was fought, of two years' duration, to find means by which it could be stamped out. But the effort was in vain. The chestnut blight has baffled all efforts to hold it in check, or to end its evil progress. It was also in the Zoölogical Park that the hickory-bark borer was vigorously attacked for the first time in the vicinity of New York.

In the summer of 1912, I made a few notes of the ravages of insects in progress at that time, under my observation, and of the efforts that were being made to stop them. Here is the memorandum:

July 12:—The bag insects, in thousands, are devouring the leaves of the locusts and maples.

The elm beetles are at work on the foliage of the elms; and spraying operations are in progress.

The hickory-bark borers are slaughtering the hickories; and even some Park people are neglecting to take the measures necessary to stop them.

The tent caterpillars are being burned.

The aphides (plant-lice) are destroying the tops of the white potatoes in the school garden of the New York University, just as the potato-beetles do.

The codling-moth larvæ are already at work on the apples.

The leaves affected by the witch-hazel gall-insect are being cut off and burned.

This schedule did not attempt to take into account any save the most conspicuous of the insect pests that were in evidence on that one day. It is only a faint reflection of the hand-to-hand fight that tree-owners and tree-protectors are called upon to wage each year against insect enemies.

In order that we may approach our subject in a thoroughly chastened and humble frame of mind, let us make a brief survey of the damage inflicted in a stated period upon agriculture, horticulture and forestry in the United States.

In 1903, the Department of Agriculture very wisely ordered a group of its expert investigators and statisticians to examine and to report upon the annual damage inflicted by insects upon the leading industrial interests of our country. The investigation was directed by Mr. C. L. Marlatt, and the results were published in the departmental Year-book of 1904. It is no exaggeration to say that they profoundly astonished the public. The figures representing damages were arrived at by obtaining estimates of the percentage of loss for 1903 to the various plant industries of the nation and to forests, and from the known value of the various crops the amount of damage to each was figured out. So far as I am aware, the accuracy of the published figures never has been disputed. The annual loss to the various crops ranges from 10 to 20 per cent. The following is the statement of annual losses on farm and forest products chargeable to insect pests:

Natural forests and forest products,		$100,000,000.
Cereals,	10 per cent,	200,000,000.
Hay,	10 per cent,	53,000,000.
Cotton,	10 per cent,	60,000,000.
Tobacco,	10 per cent,	5,300,000.
Truck crops,	20 per cent,	53,000,000.
Sugar,	10 per cent,	5,000,000.
Fruits,	20 per cent,	27,000,000.
Farm forests,	10 per cent,	11,000,000.
Miscellaneous crops,	10 per cent,	5,800,000.
Total,		$520,100,000.

The losses inflicted by insect pests on forests and forest products were estimated by Dr. A. D. Hopkins, the departmental special agent in charge of forest insect investigations. Every person who will read, or even examine, Dr. Hopkins's writings on his special subject surely will be convinced that of all men in America he is best qualified to speak with authority on that subject. His estimate of $100,000,000 as the annual loss to timber interests covers the losses from insect damages to standing timber, and also to forest products, both crude and manufactured.

Dr. Hopkins's work on the bark-beetles of North America is, to the layman, a startling revelation. For example, it shows that, leaving all other insects out of consideration, there are seven species of bark-beetles whose depredations cover the whole area of the coniferous forests of the United States. Each particularly valuable species of spruce and pine has its particular curse, from the Engelmann spruce bark-beetle of the far Northwest to the southern pine-beetle of Georgia and Florida. The deadly seven are as follows, and their areas of destruction are indicated by their names:

> Western pine-beetle,
> Montana pine-beetle,
> Engelmann spruce-beetle,
> Douglas fir-beetle,
> Southern pine-beetle,
> Black Hills beetle,
> Eastern spruce-beetle.

These species cover all the areas of coniferous forests in the United States.

Corn.—Of the cereal crops, corn is destroyed,—root, stem, leaves and fruit,—by the following insects: chinch-bug, corn-root worm, bill-bug, wire-worm, boll-worm or ear-worm, cutworm, army-worm, stalk-worm, grasshopper and plant-lice,—in all about fifty important species. Of all the cereal crops, *Wheat* is the one that suffers most severely from insects. Its three deadliest enemies are the chinch-bug, Hessian fly and plant-louse. In the year 1900, the Hessian fly caused, in the states of Ohio and Indiana alone, the loss of 2,577,000 acres of wheat!

The Hay and Forage crops are attacked by locusts, grasshoppers, army-worms, cutworms, webworms, small grass-worms and leaf-hoppers. Some of these pests are so small, and work so insidiously, that even the farmer is prone to overlook their existence. The 10 per cent annual shrinkage in these crops was declared to be "a minimum estimate."

Cotton.—The great enemies of the cotton-planter are the cotton-boll weevil, the boll-worm, and the leaf-worm: but there are others that do serious damage. In 1904 the loss from the boll-weevil alone, and chiefly in Texas, was estimated at $20,000,000. Before the use of arsenical poisons, the leaf-worm caused an annual loss of from $20,-000,000 to $30,000,000, but during recent years that total has been greatly reduced.

Fruit.—The insects that destroy our fruit crops attack every portion of the tree and its fruit. The woolly aphis attacks the roots; the trunk and limbs are preyed upon by millions of plant-lice, scale-insects and borers; the leaves are devastated by the all-devouring leaf-worms, canker-worms and tent-caterpillars, while the fruit itself is attacked by the curculio, codling-moth and apple-maggot. By the annual expenditure of about $8,000,000 in cash in the spraying of apple-trees, the destructiveness of the codling-moth and curculio have been greatly reduced; but of course that great sum must be set down as a *total loss* to the farmers and consumers, in addition to a shrinkage of $12,000,000 in the annual crop from insect ravages that could not be prevented.

Now, in view of the foregoing, is it, or is it not, worth while for serious-minded men to do their very utmost, continuously, to protect from foolish and brutal slaughter man's only allies in the insect war, the insect-eating birds? Let us see what we have to gain by such protection.

Fortunately for the producers and consumers of the United States, our Department of Agriculture has made thorough and exhaustive investigations into the food-habits of our insect-eating birds, and the results are available to the world. These results have been obtained by collecting a large series of specimens of each bird species investigated, covering the entire year, and carefully examining the contents of each stomach.

There is one important factor, however, that those investigations have not taken into account, and that is, *the enormous number of insects, or rather of insect larvæ, that are consumed by each nesting pair of birds in rearing its young.* Each pair of insectivorous birds that breeds in our country gives "hostages to fortune" in the shape of an ever hungry nestful of young birds. Irrevocably it commits itself to a line of activities in insect destruction that is almost beyond belief. It is no uncommon thing for a pair of perching birds to bring insect food to their young 100, 200 or even 250 times in a day. Fortunate indeed is the farmer on whose insect-ridden premises the warblers, phoebe birds, vireos, thrushes or catbirds make their nests and rear their hungry broods.

It is well that the experts of the Department of Agriculture have put before us names and figures to reveal the work of the insectivorous birds. The birds do their entomological work so quietly and unostentatiously that until the records were given us, we had no adequate conception of the extent or the value of the work annually accomplished for us by our feathered friends. The average farmer notices most particularly the birds that damage his cherries and grapes. The average friend of the birds notices particularly those whose songs appeal to him, and it is only the confirmed bird-lover who is willing to make the observations that count.

I heartily wish that every forester in America could have seen what I saw no longer ago than last September in the Berkshire Hills when the song-birds were beginning to move southward. By accident of position, I saw a flock of perhaps twenty-five warblers go through the top of a large oak tree, starting on one side and working through to the other. Those little gray sprites literally combed the foliage of that tree-top for insects, almost leaf by leaf. It was done so quietly that only a watchful eye would have noticed it. Many other times, however, I have watched warblers hunting through foliage with a thoroughness that is highly gratifying to a hater of noxious insects.

There are five groups of birds of special value to us because of the insects they consume; and they will be named in what we believe to be the order of their importance. They are:

> The song-birds,
> The tree-climbers,
> The swallows and swifts,
> The shore-birds,
> The grouse and quail.

To these are to be added a number of miscellaneous species of special value, such as the goat-suckers, certain small hawks, and a few ducks, egrets, herons and ibises.

The Song-Birds of themselves alone form a mighty host. The great family of *Warblers* heads the list, both in number of species and in static efficiency. Except the humming-birds, they are the smallest of the passerine order, and the forms and colors of many of the species are so very inconspicuous that only the sharp eye will notice their tiny gray forms as they quietly flit or glide, a yard at each move, through the foliage that they are combing out. Their work is mostly in the tops of the trees. The high-water mark in insect destruction is reached by these birds. Bulletin No. 44 of the Department of Agriculture gives the results of an exhaustive examination of 3,398 warbler stomachs, from seventeen species, and the result shows 95 per cent of insect food,—mostly bad insects, too,—

and 5 per cent of vegetable food. What more than that can any forester ask of a bird?

The *Baltimore Oriole* stands very high as a destroyer of insects; and incidentally its nest is the most wonderful example of bird architecture to be found in North America. In May, insects make up 90 per cent of the food of this bird. For the entire year, insects constitute 83.4 per cent, and vegetable food only 16.6 per cent of its bill of fare.

The *Meadow-Lark* is one of the most valuable of the birds that persistently frequent farming regions. During the insect season, 90 per cent of its food consists of insects, and during the year as a whole, insects make up 73 per cent.

Even the *Crow Blackbird,* with a reputation not of the best, finds 27 per cent of its food in the ranks of our insect enemies, and it has been fully acquitted of the ancient charge of nest-robbing.

Perhaps the most interesting single exhibit in all the long list of good services of insectivorous birds is that which brings together the known enemies and destroyers of the devastating cotton-boll weevil. This is really a southern exhibit of northern birds, and directly concerns half a dozen states of the Gulf coast of the South, states which we long have been earnestly exhorting to consider the economic value of birds, and stop within their borders the slaughter of the crop-protecting species.

The list of birds that wage war on the cotton-boll weevil contains *fifty-two species,* some of which

QUAIL SLAUGHTER IN TEXAS, ACCORDING TO LAW

And the Quail is a great destroyer of the cotton-boll weevil, which in Texas is a very destructive pest!

make a specialty of the weevil, while others take it incidentally, in the course of each day's work. The list is far too long to quote in full, but to show the gallant manner in which a great number of bird families, and orders also, are endeavoring to do their part in the weevil warfare, we will offer a few items from the list. We notice the following species: six orioles, six sparrows, one goatsucker, one martin, five swallows, and various fly-catchers, wrens, blackbirds, the killdeer plover, titlark, meadow-lark and quail. Of these birds, the martin, swallows and nighthawk capture the weevils while they are flying high in the air; the song-birds take them from the cotton plants, and the quail and meadow-lark glean them near the ground. A farmer of Beeville, Texas, once reported as follows: "The bob-whites shot in this vicinity had their crops *filled* with the boll-weevils." Another Texas farmer reported his "cotton-fields full of quail, and an entire absence of weevils."

And yet, in spite of all this, I received not long since, from Texas, a photograph showing a large automobile almost concealed from end to end by a thick mantle of dead quail.

For a change of scenery, let us glance for a moment at the bird enemies of the codling-moth, the greatest destroyer of northern apples. This list of thirty-six species also shows a great variety of birds on one particular firing-line, in which several different orders and thirteen families are represented. Consider this array of birds that devour the larvæ of the codling-moth to an important extent: six species of woodpeckers, two of fly-catchers, three jays, two blackbirds, one oriole, two sparrows, two warblers, six chickadees, nuthatches and creepers, one towhee, one cardinal, one king-bird, one grosbeak, one bunting, one swallow, a kinglet, bush-tit, robin and bluebird.

In some places these birds have been credited with having destroyed from 66 to 85 per cent of the hibernating codling-moth larvæ.

But we must return to the consideration of the other important groups of insect-eating birds. Undoubtedly every student of forestry will be more interested in the work of Group No. 2, the tree-climbing birds, than in any other, because nearly every member of that group is itself a forest con-servator of long standing. It is at all times a great pleasure to consider the woodpeckers, nuthatches, chickadees and creepers.

Of all man's numerous feathered friends and allies, the woodpeckers appeal to me most strongly. I admire the courage which prompts them to stay with us throughout the long and dreary winter, and take their chances of finding food and shelter. I admire both the indomitable industry and the mechanical skill with which they dig into the bark, and even the trunk-wood of trees, in grim pursuit of the insects that need to be destroyed. The woodpecker is a true sportsman, not an angler.

He does not wait upon the convenience of the game, but he goes after it,—digging, gouging and drilling until the enemy is finally brought to bay, impaled on a tongue that is a living spear of many barbs and dragged forth to its doom.

It is the woodpecker that stays with us in November and sticks to his job whence all but him have fled. When in midwinter you slowly plow your way through a foot of snow in the silent and desolated woods, and hear overhead the sound of digging and gouging in wood, you know that you are not wholly alone. Watch for falling chips, then look aloft, and you will see a downy or hairy woodpecker busily working away on an insect-ridden area of tree-trunk, doing work for you and me. When a woodpecker beats a rolling tattoo on the hard outer shell of a dead limb, filling a quarter-mile circle with marvelously rapid sound waves, he is not then digging for insects. He is showing off. He is playing to the galleries, literally, and endeavoring to attract a mate. When he really *works,* he wastes no time in theatrical drumming, and you must listen sharply in order to locate him.

One of the permanent regrets of my life is that nature has not yet produced for the hardwood forests of North America a woodpecker as large as a condor, with a steel-tipped beak that can successfully drill through and split open the bark of the shell-bark hickory, and bring the hickory-bark borer to justice.

The *Downy Woodpecker* is one of the smaller of our North American species, but of insect destroyers it is literally the little giant. Seventy-four per cent of its food consists of insects injurious to trees, and 25 per cent only is of vegetable origin. The *Hairy Woodpecker* is a close rival of the downy, in size, color, habits and dynamic force. Its official record is 68 per cent of insect food. Both these species remain in this region throughout the year.

After the woodpeckers, the nuthatches and brown creepers render valuable service to trees by going over their trunks inch by inch, picking off and devouring the scale-insects, bark-lice and any other surface pests that can be captured without digging. Their slender beaks are like tiny forceps for all crevices, but they are totally unfit for the gouge and gimlet work in which the woodpecker excels.

The pert little *Black-Capped Chickadee* also lives with us all winter, and it seems to be a bird of infinite leisure. Rarely will you see it at work. When you approach, it devotes all its time to visiting with you, and so long as you remain near it, its interest in you never flags. Inasmuch as it feeds upon tree-inhabiting insects, it is certain that it performs its small share of tree-protection work.

In view of the very great value of the woodpeckers, their steady disappearance has been noted with increasing regret and alarm. Ten years ago, these birds were far more numerous in southern

New York than they now are. I am quite certain that their disappearance has been caused by the slaughter of them for food, in the North by the Italians, and in the South by negroes. In October, 1905, two special game wardens of the New York Zoölogical Society arrested in the northern part of New York City two Italian guerrillas of destruction who had in their possession forty-three insectivorous birds, five of which were woodpeckers.

Now that the federal migratory bird law is in force, and the strong hand of the national government is to be put forth everywhere in behalf of such birds as these, we are given new hope for the stoppage of the slaughter of our most useful birds, and the return of the millions that have vanished.

The group of *Martins and Swallows* forms a clearly cut avian order, every member of which is a potent force in insect destruction. Like the nighthawk, they operate in mid-air, chasing flying insects in full flight, and devouring them on the wing. They operate in a field of activity that is inaccessible to man, and the marvelous perfection with which they perform their special function is almost enough to compel us to go back to the old belief in special creation.

The insectivorous habits of the martins and the swallows have long been known. Even the dullest swamp-mucker who ever carried a gun could not by any possibility shut his eyes and his brain to the spectacle presented by these graceful birds hunting

insects in mid-air, or long remain in ignorance of
their food habits. In the South, the martins and
swallows are among the most useful and valuable
of all birds in the destruction of the cotton-boll
weevil. It is their peculiar function to catch the
weevils as they make long flights, when leaving the
cotton-fields in search of hiding-places in which to
winter, or more congenial spots in which to continue their work of devastation.

In view of all this, does it not seem positively
incredible that intelligent white men in the South,
men who can read and write, and who popularly
are classed as "sportsmen," can be so stupid and
so wicked as to shoot purple martins as "game"!
And yet it is reported that throughout sections of
the South, the shooting of the martin is (or until
recently has been) a common practice. Probably
this is the reason why the purple martin is now so
rare in the North, and survives in only a few
localities. Over thousands of square miles of its
former summer home it is extinct. It is such exasperating doings as these that have driven some
of us into the ranks of the so-called wild-life
"fanatics," there to wage ceaseless warfare against
the abominable practices of the guerrillas of
destruction.

Fortunately all species of the martins and
swallows are migratory, and our hope for their
survival is now renewed by the migratory bird law.

The Shore-Birds.—We now have reached the

order of shore-birds, concerning which a strange condition now exists. Forty years ago, aye, even thirty years ago, many members of this group of sixty conspicuous bird species were scattered throughout the length and breadth of our country east of the great plains and west of the Sierra Nevada Mountains. The jack-snipe, woodcock, killdeer plover, the curlews, dowitchers and others spread from the Atlantic coast to Nebraska and Kansas, and everyone knew them.

To-day, in practical effect, the shore-birds of the United States are limited to a remnant along the Atlantic shore line, and another remnant along the Pacific coast. At long intervals between, in little pockets as it were, a few snipe and woodcock still survive, but as representatives of the great blanket of shore-birds that once was spread over our country, they do not amount to anything more than pitiful samples. To-day, when you say to your neighbor that "our shore-birds are vanishing, and need quick protection," the chances are that he will look at you with a puzzled expression, and ask in all sincerity, "Just what *are* shore-birds?" This has actually occurred repeatedly in my experience during the past two years. It is a fact that to-day our shore-birds need an introduction to the American people at large, their natural protectors.

If we are asked to describe the order of shore-birds, in a few words, we may say that it contains the long-legged, slender-billed, plainly colored

birds of small or very moderate size, that frequent
the shores of all bodies of open water, large and
small, salt and fresh, and also many regions of open
plains and prairies.   The group embraces the
plovers, curlews, sandpipers, phalaropes, avocets,
dowitchers, woodcock and snipe; in all about sixty
North American species. On the farms and prairies
of the eastern half of the United States, the species
most commonly seen thirty years ago were the
killdeer plover, jack-snipe and curlew.

Until about four years ago, the shore-birds were
regarded as of value only for food, and on that
basis they have long been relentlessly pursued.   In
1911, a circular issued by the Department of Agriculture, written by Prof. W. L. McAtee, brought
prominently to notice the astonishing fact that the
shore-birds are of immense value as insect destroyers, performing services that are not performed by any other birds.   This revelation has
completely changed the status of these universally
persecuted birds, and created a demand for their
adequate protection.

From Professor McAtee's circular No. 79, we
quote the following significant paragraph:

Throughout the eastern United States, shore-birds are *fast
vanishing*. While formerly numerous species swarmed along
the Atlantic coast and in the prairie regions, many of them
have been so reduced that extermination seems imminent.   The
black-bellied plover, or beetle-head, which occurred along the
Atlantic seaboard in great numbers years ago, is now seen

only as a straggler.   The golden plover, once exceedingly
abundant east of the Great Plains, is now rare.   Vast hordes of
long-billed dowitchers formerly wintered in Louisiana; now
they occur only in infrequent flocks of only a half dozen or
less.   The Eskimo curlew within the last decade has probably
been exterminated, and the other curlews have been greatly
reduced.   In fact, all the larger species of shore-birds have
suffered severely.   So adverse to shore-birds are present conditions, *the wonder is that any escape!*   In both fall and
spring they are shot along the whole route of their migration,
north and south.   Their habit of decoying readily and persistently, coming back in flocks to the decoys again and again,
in spite of murderous volleys, greatly lessens their chances of
escape. . . .   Shore-birds have been hunted until only a
remnant of their once vast numbers is left.   Their limited
powers of reproduction, coupled with the natural vicissitudes
of the breeding period, make their increase slow, and peculiarly
expose them to danger of extermination.

In the struggle that was made for the passage of
the federal migratory bird law, the claims of the
shore-birds, and the interests benefited by them,
were strongly set forth.   A demand was registered
for a five-year close season on all species of shore-
birds inhabiting or passing through the United
States.   This demand was redoubled after the
enactment of the law, and while the detailed regulations were being framed.   By strongly insisting
upon the giving of the whole loaf, fifty-four out of
our sixty species of shore-birds actually *did* secure
the five-year period of protection that was demanded.   The species left open to slaughter were
the woodcock, jack-snipe, greater and lesser yellow-

legs, golden plover and black-breasted plover. The unhappy six, one of them already so rare as to be out of the reckoning, were literally thrown to the lions of the arena, in order that the baffled rage of the men who love bird slaughter might not become too great for the nation at large to endure.

Personally, I never could see the slightest sport in shooting any of the shore-birds of the seashore; but to the sandpiper sportsmen those foolish little birds are all great game. Fancy, if you please, a grown man in a fifteen-dollar hunting suit, carrying a ten-dollar gun and a one-dollar license, shooting tiny sandpipers as "game," to eat as "food"! It is difficult to imagine the frame of mind or the code of ethics of the typical sandpiper sportsman; but the class exists and persists, and it is to be reckoned with.

To one who never has paused to consider the economic value of the shore-birds—and this subject is so very new there is much excuse for unfamiliarity with it—the value of these birds as insect destroyers is positively astounding. I regret that it is impossible to offer here more than a brief and inadequate impression of that value. The shore-bird diet includes quantities of such notorious insect pests as the following: Rocky Mountain locust, and other injurious grasshoppers; army-worms, cutworms, cabbage-worms, the cotton-worm, cotton-boll weevil, clover-leaf weevil, clover-root curculio, rice-weevil, corn bill-bugs, wireworms, corn-leaf beetles, cucumber beetles, white grubs, Texas fever-tick, horse-flies and mosquitoes. Of mosquitoes, the shore-birds are the most important bird enemies known to us.

Let us take, by way of illustration, a short series of cases reported by the Department of Agriculture, involving the destruction of the dreaded Rocky Mountain locust in the state of Nebraska, a region of rich farms and artificial groves.

9 killdeer plover stomachs contained an average of 28 locusts each.

11 semi-palmated plover stomachs contained an average of 38 locusts each.

16 mountain plover stomachs contained an average of 45 locusts each.

11 jack-snipe stomachs contained an average of 37 locusts each.

22 upland plover stomachs contained an average of 36 locusts each.

10 long-billed curlew stomachs contained an average of 48 locusts each.

The conditions described above were the result of an unusual abundance of the locusts preyed upon. At all times, wherever grasshoppers are available, they are sought by shore-birds of at least twenty-four species, as follows: seven plovers, six sandpipers, two snipes, one phalarope, the avocet, stilt, woodcock, dowitcher, long-billed curlew, godwit, yellow-legs and turnstone.

Nine species of shore-birds eat mosquitoes.

Eight species devour the larvæ of the crane flies that are so destructive to grass and wheat.

The beautiful and once very common killdeer plover and the spotted sandpiper feed upon the army-worm and other pests of the grain-fields.

Cutworms are eaten by the avocet, woodcock, two sandpipers and two plovers; and one of the latter, the killdeer, destroys the cotton-worm, cotton cutworm, tobacco-worm and tomato-worm. The detestable bill-bug, one of the special enemies of corn, is eaten by eight species of shore-birds. It is reported from Corpus Christi, Texas, that upland plovers are industrious in following the plough, and eating the grubs that destroy garden vegetables, corn and cotton crops.

An observer in Fall River, Massachusetts, has reported the following facts regarding the spotted sandpiper: "Three pairs nested in a young orchard behind my house, adjacent to my garden. I did not see them once go to the shore for food (shore about 1,500 feet away), but I did see them many times make faithful search of my garden for cutworms, spotted squash-bugs and green flies. Cutworms and cabbage-worms were their special prey. After the young could fly, they still kept at work in my garden, and showed no inclination to go to the shore until about August 15. They and a flock of quails just over the wall helped me wonderfully."

And yet, let us add, there are grown men in this country, tens of thousands of them, who think it is

sport to shoot the useful spotted sandpiper, a bird
so small that it takes at least four of them to make
a respectable dinner portion.

I am still claiming that every species of shore-
bird in America now is entitled to at least a five-
year close season, as a matter of justice, common
sense and common decency. I regard only two
species of shore-birds as legitimate game, at any
time, even when they are generally plentiful.
These are the woodcock and jack-snipe. If I had
my will, all other species should forever be immune
from slaughter; first, because of the good they do;
second, because of the element of interest they add
to shores and interior lands; and third, because as
game-birds few of them taste good and the quantity
of food they furnish never amounted to an item
worthy of serious consideration.

The advocates of shore-bird killing—and there
are many—will tell us that "there are thousands of
them," of various species, to be found on the south
shore of Long Island, and elsewhere on the Atlantic coast. Last spring on a cold, raw and rainy day,
a shore-bird sportsman took me to Great South
Bay, during the spring flight northward. It was
on May 27. In spite of bad weather conditions we
steamed to and fro, in and out, around and about
through that great watery labyrinth until we saw at
least 2,000 shore-birds, of nine species. Had the
day been fine and clear we would undoubtedly have
seen many more.

The exhibition was gratifying, not because there were so many birds that a single gunner would have enough birds of *his* gun, but because we found so much seed stock for the bringing back of those species. But mark you what those birds represented. They represented the massing together during the two, three or four weeks of the annual migration northward to their breeding-grounds, of *a very considerable portion* of the stock of shore-birds of *our whole Atlantic coast!* Those birds, as we saw them, were at one of their most necessary resting-places and feeding-grounds,—an area which in any event should forever be to them a sanctuary and an inviolable refuge.

The remaining shore-birds of North America are barely sufficient in number to save the order Limicolæ as a whole from extermination on this continent. The five-year remedy for fifty-four species has been applied not soon enough to save the Eskimo curlew, the golden plover, and possibly others. But the regulation that went into effect on October 1, under the terms of the federal migratory bird law, is a long step in the right direction. Without it, we would have gone on vainly appealing to the various states until all the birds of an entire order of sixty would have been blotted out, literally before the eyes of the friends who sought to save them.

The Upland Game-Birds.—The conservation of our upland game-birds, the grouse and quail, rests

on two widely different necessities. The grouse
should be saved and increased as a food supply, and
the bob-white quail should be protected because of
its value as a destroyer of insects and the seeds of
noxious weeds. Let us first consider the quail,
because it is nearest.

Probably 99 per cent of the farmers of this country, and 100 per cent of the sportsmen and gunners
outside New York, regard the common *Virginia
Quail,* or *Bob-White,* as a bird of no economic
value save when it is shot and eaten. To this enormous army of enemies, the bird is only a question of
meat ounces on the table. And yet, thanks to the
painstaking investigations of Mrs. Nice, of Clark
University, and Professor Judd, of the United
States Department of Agriculture, we now know
that for the smaller pests of the farm the bob-white
is the most wonderful engine of destruction ever
put together of flesh and blood. I think it is fairly
beyond question that of all the birds that influence
the fortunes of the farmers and fruit-growers of
North America, *the common quail is the most
valuable!*

It remains on the farm throughout the year.
When insects are most numerous, bob-white devotes to them his entire time. He destroys them
during sixteen to eighteen hours of the summer day.
When the insects are gone, he turns his attention
to the weeds that are striving to seed down the
farmer's fields for another year. He consumes, as

palatable food, the seeds of 129 species of weeds; and the quantity that one bird can consume in one day is almost beyond belief. Ten thousand seeds for one bird's daily ration is a small quantity, and far below the average of what a healthy adult bird requires. To kill weeds on the farm costs money,— hard cash that the farmer has earned by toil, or labor of cash value which he himself bestows. Does the average farmer ever put forth any strenuous efforts to protect from poachers and other enemies the quail that work so well and so faithfully for him? The exceptional farmer does; the average farmer does not.

All that the *average* farmer thinks of the quail, even those in his own coveys, is as so much meat for his table.

A list of the 129 species of weeds whose seeds are eaten by the bob-white looks like a botanical rogues' gallery. Conspicuous in it are such old enemies as the pigweed, smartweed, beggar-tick, foxtail, burdock, barnyard grass, crab grass, ragweed and plantain. It has been calculated that if in Virginia and North Carolina there were four bob-whites to every square mile, and each bird ate one ounce of weed seeds per day, from September 1 to April 30, the total amount consumed in those two states would be 1,341 tons.

As a destroyer of insects it would seem that the common quail deserves the first place. We know of no other species whose appetite covers so wide a variety of insect food. It is known that this bird consumes 145 different species of insects, and the list includes all the notorious insect pests of the farm and orchard save the few that live and work high up, beyond the reach of a bird that lives on the ground. However, the quail's repertoire includes the codling-moth, the garden caterpillars, flies, mosquitoes, plant-lice, cotton-boll weevil and a host of others.

While it is impossible to take time to name many of the insect species involved, we can offer a summary of the quail's insect food, as follows:

Grasshoppers and locusts	13 species
Bugs	24 species
Leaf-hoppers and plant-lice	6 species
Moths, caterpillars, cutworms, etc.	19 species
Flies	8 species
Beetles	61 species
Ants, wasps and slugs	8 species
Miscellaneous species	6 species
Total	145 species

It would be possible to go on at greater length, piling fact upon fact, to demonstrate the value of the quail to the farming and fruit-growing interests; but why burden the subject with unnecessary proof? We are not now attempting to cover the quail situation of the Pacific coast, which for various reasons forms a chapter by itself, and needs to be considered independently. Regarding the situation everywhere east of the Rocky Mountains, should it not be perfectly clear to every logical mind that the only rational course to pursue is to give the bob-white quail, everywhere, close seasons of five or ten years, or until they become so numerous as to be destructive to valuable crops? The quail needs a million champions; but instead of having them, it is annually beset by more than a million gunners.

Instead of universal protection, to-day we find only three states maintaining a five-year close season on their quail. Those states are New York, Oklahoma and Kansas. If there are others doing likewise, I have overlooked them. Throughout fully nine-tenths of the range of the quail, it is harassed and persecuted by men, dogs, automatic and pump guns, automobiles and public sentiment. In Iowa an unwise state game warden blocked the passage of a five-year protection law for quail on the fantastic ground that if the bill should become a law, the sportsmen of the state of Iowa would be so furiously angry that they would exterminate all the remaining quail in revenge! That idea may fairly be regarded as the greatest invention of the age in the line of conservation.

As yet, the average American farmer is sound asleep on the quail question. Whether it will be possible to arouse him, and induce him to rise in his might and demand long protection for his best feathered friend, is now a question before the house.

It can not be answered by a roll-call, but it could be answered by vigorous action.

Our treatment of the grouse of the East and the Middle West is a sore subject. Draw a line around the former range of our old friend, the pinnated grouse or prairie-chicken, and you will include the hog-and-corn area of the United States. That, also, is *the area of the most complete local extermination of wild life, both birds and mammals!* It includes the states of Ohio, Indiana, Illinois, Iowa, Missouri, Kansas, Nebraska, Kentucky and Tennessee. In that hog-and-corn belt you will find more spring shooting, more sale of game, more extermination and less real wild-life protection than in any other area of the United States.

On the island of Mauritius, it was swine that exterminated the dodo. In the United States, hogs and game extermination still go hand in hand. Since the days of the dodo, however, a new species of swine has been developed. It is now widely known as the game-hog, and its existence and its activities have been officially recognized by both bench and bar. Although the name is rude and jarring, it is now a necessary term; and it has come to stay.

Take the case of Ohio as a horrible example,—a state once abundantly stocked with a great variety and a great number of game birds and mammals. I think that Ohio comes the nearest of all the states to being gameless. With but slight exceptions, her laws are not wholly bad; but in the breasts of her citizens the desire to kill is so strong, and the majority of her gunners are so thoroughly selfish about their so-called "rights" to kill, that the game has ruthlessly been *swept away according to law!* The state is a striking example of the deplorable results of *legalized* slaughter. Her sportsmen will not have a law forbidding the use in hunting of the automatic shot-gun. Oh, no! They say, "Limit the bag, shorten the open season, and the species of the gun won't matter."

As an answer to that proposition, we will file this list of game birds and mammals that already have been totally exterminated in the state of Ohio:

Pinnated grouse,	Elk,
Passenger pigeon,	Black bear,
Wild turkey,	Puma,
Pileated woodpecker,	Lynx,
Carolina parrakeet,	Gray wolf,
Bison,	Beaver,
White-tailed deer,	Otter.

Eight species of valuable birds are reported as *"threatened* with extinction" in the near future; but we will not take time to name them. One of them is the quail.

But to return to the grouse.

Pinnated Grouse.—Unless there is a swift and complete change in the treatment accorded the remnants of pinnated grouse, sage-grouse and sharp-tailed grouse, many men now in this audience will live to see the day when all three of those fine species will become totally extinct throughout this country. Their extinguishment at this late day through human greed and selfishness will be a national disgrace, second to the disgrace of the American bison only because the birds are of less importance to the country at large.

To the states that still possess remnant flocks of pinnated grouse—notably Minnesota, the Dakotas, Nebraska, Kansas and Oklahoma—we have appealed for a five-year close season; but thus far in vain. The noble-minded, big-hearted "sportsmen" (!) of those states refuse to accede to the demand, and the lawmakers, who care a hundred times more about reëlection than for state game, are afraid to act against the wishes of the so-called "leading organizations of sportsmen."

In the first instance, the upland game-birds of the Middle West were slaughtered, wholesale, by market-hunters in the *absence* of law. Now they are being slaughtered and exterminated by "sportsmen" gunners *in accordance with law,*—because the open seasons continue, and because there are about ten guns and one hundred cartridges against each surviving bird. The gunners and state lawmakers of the Middle West sullenly refuse to hear and heed the lesson of the heath-hen or eastern prairie-chicken, which reached a point so low that finally even ten-year close seasons could not bring it back.

Without a quick and thorough reform, that history is destined to be reënacted between the Mississippi and the Rocky Mountains, and at least three fine species will totally disappear even while the world is crying "Shame!" It is useless to talk of the value of those three grouse with their annihilation actually taking place before our eyes! The situation is too exasperating for words. We labored hard with the Department of Agriculture to have the pinnated grouse—which *is a migratory bird*—included in the protection of the federal migratory bird law; but the hostility of the game-killers of the pinnated grouse territory was feared so much that for the present that grouse is left to its fate at the hands of the states that it has the misfortune to inhabit.

The eastern ruffed grouse, often miscalled the "pheasant," is the only grouse of the United States concerning which we can at present indulge even a ray of hope. It inhabits timber and brush and rocky hillsides, it does not live in large flocks like the grouse of prairie countries, and it can not be run down with dogs, camp-wagons and automobiles as the prairie grouse are. It is damaged during the breeding season by roaming bird-dogs, but cats do not seriously affect it, and a bad shot seldom kills it. It is to other grouse what the white-tailed deer is to other hoofed game—a timber-loving skulker that will live longest because it knows best how to hide and to escape when attacked. It is now estimated by a Connecticut state game commissioner that during 1913 the 27,000 licensed gunners of Connecticut killed 60,000 ruffed grouse.

Hawks and Owls.—It is impossible to complete a discussion of the North American birds useful to man without an adequate reference to the services of certain birds of prey.

Men who never have fought a numerous and aggressive population of rats and mice do not know the bitterness of that unequal warfare; but

> " The toad beneath the harrow knows
> Exactly where each tooth-point goes!"

The rat works while men sleep; and everything that he can chew is open to destruction by him. When grain, fruit and vegetables fail, or pall upon the murine palate, the rat joyously attacks eggs, poultry and meat supplies generally. The making of farm products safe from hungry rats is a maddening proposition. What, then, should be the attitude of every farmer toward a bird like the barn owl, that lives on mice and rats, and is abundantly able, by nature, to beat the nocturnal destroyers at their own game? We would say in answer that *Strix flammea,* not *Ceres,* should be the patron saint of the farmer, and that in his eyes the barn owl should be ten times more sacred than the peacock is to a Hindoo.

Forty years ago, if tradition speaks truly, no one would easily have believed it possible that any of the hawks and owls of the United States were otherwise than highly injurious to man, and therefore deserving of instant death. But we live and learn. The shot-guns, scalpels and microscopes of the Department of Agriculture have placed the hawks and owls, all save five or six, in an entirely different class from that which had been theirs from the beginning. To-day it is only the benighted states of America that fail to protect the hawks and owls,—all save a very few species that will be considered, on a later occasion, as pests.

The valuable services rendered by the useful hawks and owls consist in the destruction of rats, mice, gophers, shrews and moles. Those small and elusive mammals must be kept in check by their natural enemies, especially the nocturnal birds of prey and the small carnivorous mammals.

By way of illustration, take the record of a famous pair of *Barn Owls* that once nested in one of the towers of the Smithsonian building at Washington. Conditions were such that the pellets of indigestible animal matter disgorged by those two birds were accidentally preserved for an entire year, and thereby yielded a valuable record. Two hundred pellets were collected, consisting of bones, hair and feathers, and it was found that they contained 453 skulls which represented the following mammals: 225 meadow mice, 179 house mice, 20 rats, 2

Ptarmigan Slaughter in the Absence of Law. Yukon Ter., 1913

Part of a lot of 3000 birds killed by miners and railroad men at Pueblo, near White Horse.

pine mice, 20 shrews, 6 jumping mice and 1 mole. The collection contained the skull of one bird only, a vesper sparrow.

The *Long-Eared Owl* has a record for rats and mice very similar to that of the barn owl; scores of mice, rats and shrews destroyed, but alas! too many birds, also! Its nearest relative, the *Short-Eared Owl,* is a bird of precisely similar habits.

Formerly the *Red-Shouldered* and *Red-Tailed Hawks* were universally known as "chicken hawks," hated accordingly by the farmer and shot whenever possible. Now it is known that those hawks rarely feed on domestic poultry, and that they devour so many wild mice and rats that they are decidedly beneficial to man and worthy of protection.

In 1885, the rural feeling against hawks and owls reached high-water mark in Pennsylvania. In response to the demands of the farmers of the state, the Pennsylvania legislature enacted a law providing a bounty of fifty cents each for the heads of hawks and owls. Naturally, great slaughter of these birds ensued. In two years, 180,000 scalps had been brought in and $90,000 had been paid out for them.

The awakening came even more swiftly than the ornithologists expected. By the end of two years from the enactment of "the hawk law," the farmers found their fields and orchards thoroughly overrun by destructive mice, rats and insects; and again they went clamoring to the legislature, this time for the quick repeal of the law. With all possible haste this was brought about; but it was estimated by competent judges that in damages to their crops "the fool hawk law" cost the farmers of the state of Pennsylvania more than $2,000,000.

The moral of this episode is that it is very dangerous to meddle with the balance of nature by a wholesale destruction of hawks and owls. There are a very few species that deserve to be destroyed, but those are now so difficult to find and so difficult to identify at gunshot distance, that only an intelligent hunter is competent to undertake their destruction and guarantee no killings by mistake. To-day the really destructive species are almost a negligible factor in wild-life economy, and I encourage no one save a bird man to go hunting for the objectionable hawks and owls. There is no longer any real necessity to provide bounties for the destruction of the few and now rare species of hawks that do more harm than good and that deserve destruction *when they are numerous.*

In conclusion, the economic value of all the insect-eating and most of the rodent-eating birds is so great that every friend of our crops and forests should insist, in season and out of season, boldly and confidently, upon the absolute and inviolate protection of all species save the few admitted to be pests deserving destruction. This proposition is not open to argument.

The American people as a whole have too long played fast and loose with their wild life. Even with our good new laws, I warn every college man in America that the situation of the birds of the United States—all save the water-fowl—is now desperate. It is gravely questionable whether it now is possible to bring back the vanished millions and once more enjoy their valuable coöperation in our endless war of self-defense against the insect world.

CHAPTER III

THE LEGITIMATE USE OF GAME BIRDS AND MAMMALS

After 30,000 years of wild-life slaughter, if we date back to the cave men of southern France who hunted and drew pictures of the mammoths and rhinoceroses of Europe, man at last is beginning to consider the rational treatment of the world's stock of game birds and quadrupeds. Perhaps one man out of every thousand—to make a very high estimate—will now admit that the finest of the beasts and birds and fishes have some rights which predatory man should respect. It must be admitted, however, that throughout the world at large, at least 99 per cent of the consideration that is now accorded wild animals is based on thoroughly selfish grounds and the desire for future benefits at the cost of their lives.

We are certain that there is now in the United States more genuine sentimental regard for wild life than can be found in any other country. In all the campaign work and the lobbying that has been done in Congress during the past fifteen years in behalf of new laws and appropriations for the better preservation of wild life, our cause has never but once been ridiculed as a sentimental cause, and very, very little has been said in debate regarding the absence of money values from the wild birds and beasts.

Up to this date, Congress has appropriated during the last seven years at least $150,000 for the founding of national bison ranges and herds, but not once has an objection been raised because the bison is no longer of economic value. On the other hand, the friends of the bison have openly declared to Congress that the movement to save the species from extinction is based entirely on sentimental grounds. This state of feeling in Congress is mentioned because it clears the atmosphere, and relieves us of the necessity of defending the sentimental aspect of our work.

It would indeed be most ungrateful to omit here a just reference to the very important part that has been played by the wild life of America in the settlement and development of our country. In fact, it is so far-reaching in extent, and so enormous in potential value, that it fairly challenges the imagination.

From the landing of the Pilgrims down to the present hour the wild game has been the mainstay and the resource against starvation of the path-finder, the settler, the prospector, and at times even the railroad-builder. In view of what the bison millions did for the Dakotas, Montana, Wyoming, Kansas and Texas, it is only right and square that

those states should now do something for the perpetual preservation of the bison species and all
other big game that needs help.

For years and years, the antelope millions of the
Montana and Wyoming grass-lands fed the scout
and Indian-fighter, freighter, cowboy and surveyor,
ranchman *and sheep-herder;* but thus far I have
yet to hear of one western state that has ever spent
one penny directly for the preservation of the
antelope!

To the colonist of the East and the pioneer of
the West, the white-tailed deer was an ever present
help in time of trouble. Without this omnipresent
animal, and the supply of good meat that each
white flag represented, the commissariat difficulties
of the settlers who won the country as far westward
as Indiana would have been many times greater
than they were. The backwoods Pilgrim's progress
was like this:

Trail, deer; cabin, deer; clearing; bear, corn,
deer; hogs, deer; cattle, wheat, independence.

And yet, how many men are there to-day, out of
our ninety millions of Americans and pseudo-
Americans, who remember with any feeling of
gratitude the part played in American history by
the white-tailed deer? Very few! How many
Americans are there in our land who now preserve
that deer for sentimental reasons, and because his
forbears were nation-builders? As a matter of
fact, are there any?

On every eastern pioneer's monument, the white-tailed deer should figure; and on those of the Great West, the bison and the antelope should be cast in enduring bronze, *"lest we forget!"*

The game-birds of America played a different part from that of the deer, antelope and bison. In the early days, shot-guns were few, and shot was scarce and dear. The wild turkey and goose were the smallest birds on which a rifleman could afford to expend a bullet and a whole charge of powder. It was for this reason that the deer, bear, bison and elk disappeared from the eastern United States while the game-birds yet remained abundant. With the disappearance of the big game came the fat steer, hog and hominy, the wheat-field, fruit-orchard and poultry galore.

The game-birds of America, as a class and a mass, have not been swept away to ward off starvation or to rescue the perishing. Even back in the sixties and seventies, very, very few men of the North thought of killing prairie-chickens, ducks and quail, snipe and woodcock, in order to keep the hunger wolf from the door. The process was too slow and uncertain; and besides, the really poor man rarely had the gun and ammunition. Instead of attempting to live on birds, he hustled for the staple food products that the soil of his own farm could produce.

First, last and nearly all the time, the game-birds of the United States as a whole have been sacrificed on the altar of Rank Luxury, to tempt appetites that were tired of fried chicken and other farm delicacies. To-day, even the average poor man hunts birds for the joy of the outing, and the pampered epicures of the hotels and restaurants buy game-birds, and eat small portions of them, solely to tempt jaded appetites. If there is such a thing as "class" legislation, it is that which permits a few sordid market-shooters to slaughter the birds of the whole people in order to sell them to a few epicures.

As the starting-point of all causes for the preservation of wild life, the men of America should agree upon what lawyers call a state of facts and the inevitable logic of the situation. Let us see if we can not evolve a code of ethics through the application of a little philosophy to the killing of game.

Fully 95 per cent of the men and boys who kill American game regard game birds and mammals only as things to be killed and eaten, to satisfy hunger. This is precisely the viewpoint of the cave man and the savage, and it has come down from the Man-with-a-Club to the Man-with-a-Gun, absolutely unchanged save for one thing: the latter sometimes is prompted to save to-day in order to slaughter more abundantly to-morrow.

Now, as a matter of fact, with the exception of the wildest regions of North America, that viewpoint is absolutely wrong. This country has reached such a stage of development and prosperity that even the poorest industrious man is able to satisfy the hunger of his family and himself without recourse to wild birds and mammals. To this rule even the poorest Florida cracker offers no exception, and it is only the outlaw and the moonshiner who regards it as necessary to live on deer and wild turkeys. In all North America there is, I venture to assert, not one mining-camp that really needs to subsist upon moose and deer and ptarmigan. It is a fixed fact that no mining-camp can endure without a well-established line of communication with the outside world, and the mere fact that moose meat and caribou steaks are a little cheaper than imported beef and bacon does not constitute an ethical reason why a valuable fauna of big game should be destroyed to increase the cash profits of Alaskan miners.

We grant that *real* prospectors and explorers are entitled to live on wild game when it becomes absolutely necessary; but beyond them this privilege should not be extended to any man or men, either white or red. The game-slaughter privileges now enjoyed by the Indians of Alaska are utterly wrong, and should be withdrawn. All Indians, and all other natives, should be compelled to observe the same game-laws as white men. They have no more inherent right to the wild game of a continent than they have to its mineral resources or its water-power.

It is now an undeniable fact that only a few of the

American people imperatively need wild game to satisfy hunger or to ward off starvation. Good food is to be had by the thrifty in great abundance, everywhere save on the last frontier. We have become a nation of epicures, eternally picking and choosing the best and choicest foods and drinks out of a bewildering array of meats, fruits, cereals and vegetables. Ninety per cent of the Americans who go hunting for game do not know what real hunger is, save by hearsay. People do not buy terrapin, and champagne, and venison, and canvas-back duck, at from $2 to $3 per portion, to satisfy real hunger. Purchased wild game is used to pamper appetites that have been worn out in the service of luxury.

We know very well that with only a few exceptions wild game is no longer necessary to the American people as food for the hungry; but at the same time an abundant supply of wild meat, killed on a conservation basis, would make a legitimate addition to the meat supply of the nation.

As sensible people, we believe that when game is sufficiently abundant, and the killing of it does not spell extermination, it is right for man to take toll of the wilds. In my opinion, the greatest value of the game birds and mammals of the United States lies, not in their meat pounds as they lie upon the table, but in the temptation that the legitimate pursuit of them annually puts before millions of desk-weary clerks, merchants, professional men and field-weary farmers to don their beloved hunting-clothes, stalk out into the haunts of nature and say, "Begone! dull care!"

There are millions of active men who are not tempted to take violent exercise in the open air unless there is a very definite object to pursue. On the other hand, a true sportsman will cheerfully expend $400 in money and $400 worth of hard labor in killing one moose in New Brunswick for a head that easily could be purchased for $75.

In the summer of 1913, an eminent and very expensive surgeon of my acquaintance spent $4,000 in money and $8,000 worth of time in hunting and killing about ten head of Alaskan big game that as food would have been worth in the open market possibly $100, but no more. The trip saved the doctor from a nervous breakdown, and the continued practice of his skill is of benefit to a large circle of afflicted humanity.

The right sort of a man who has had a fine day in the painted woods, on the bright waters of a duck-haunted bay, or in the golden stubble of September, can fill his day and his soul with six good birds just as well as with sixty. The idea that in order to be a sportsman and enjoy a fine day in the open a man must kill a wheelbarrow-load of birds, is a mistaken idea; and if persistently adhered to, it becomes vicious. The outing in the open is the thing,—not the amount of blood-stained feathers and death in the game-bag.

The time has come when every sportsman should admit that it is not wise or sportsmanlike or right to hunt wild game of any species in a locality wherein it is on the road to extermination by excessive shooting. No game should be killed more rapidly than it breeds. Shooting on any other principle means extermination; and from this grim conclusion there is no escape.

In view of the fact that over nearly all the hunting-grounds of America the wild game is being shot much more rapidly than it is breeding, the overwhelming necessity for sweeping reforms and for long close seasons that will bring back the game in abundance, should be apparent to the dullest man that ever carried a gun. In fact, we believe that the logic of the situation is quite apparent to all; but the selfish ones wish to kill as long as the game lasts, quite contemptuous of the rights of posterity.

As one who has been a sportsman when game was plentiful, I do not wish to see hunting with the gun degenerate, as it has in Italy, to the killing of sparrows and pipits and sandpipers. I wish legitimate sport to continue for five hundred years; and it is for this reason that I now insist upon long close seasons for disappearing species, in order that they may recover and come back in millions.

As an educator of public opinion and a leader of thought, what position should be assumed by the college man regarding the utilization of wild life?

What may safely be conceded and sanely carried into effect?

We must not be extremists where extremism is unnecessary; neither must we be frightened by the cry of "prohibition" that is likely to be raised against us. Let us resolutely hew to the line, let the chips fall where they will.

We hold that the best friend of the sportsman is he who resolutely seeks to prevent sport with gun and rod from becoming extinct through the failure of legitimate game.

The methods that must be applied to preserve legitimate sport resemble a painful surgical operation. No man in his senses desires a surgeon to perform half an operation, because a complete operation would be doubly painful. If an evil is to be eradicated, we wish it done thoroughly, in order that the cure may be permanent. On this basis, the saving and restoration of American game now requires of us strong and resolute action. The patient will many times wince and cry out, but we know that the only way to preserve wild life is to enable it to breed and multiply at least as rapidly as it is destroyed.

Let us therefore lay down as one of the corner-stones of wild-life conservation the principle that *no valuable wild life ever should be destroyed, for any purpose, faster than it breeds, unless it is clearly desirable that its numbers should be reduced.*

If we accept this principle as a rule of action, we can apply it literally as a blood test, in any locality on earth, and ascertain precisely the line of policy that is necessary to-day. In any given locality, ask the old residents this question: Is your game as plentiful as it was twenty years ago? This question is readily answered; and throughout the United States there are very, very few localities in which it can be answered truthfully in the affirmative. Whenever and wherever it is answered in the negative, there hunting should be suspended for five years on every species that is vanishing.

The logic of this proposition is quite unassailable; and yet, so reckless, so greedy and so destructive is the great mass of the army of life-takers, the immediate enforcement of this principle would produce throughout our country a roar of disapproval and protest that could be heard almost around the world. It is this strange and unreasoning state of fact that renders the task of the bird and mammal protectors so difficult.

The case of small game in America, and of the men who pursue it, is particularly serious, because of the fact that there are so very, very few localities in which the birds are not being killed far faster than they are breeding. The quail, grouse and shore-birds are in a very desperate state. I know of but one locality in which even a single species of upland game-bird is breeding faster than it is being killed. In the deserts of southern Arizona, Gambel's quail, a species resembling the well-known valley-quail of California, is gloriously holding its own, chiefly because its natural enemies are so few and sportsmen rarely molest it. Over thousands of square miles of creosote bushes, mesquites and cacti of various kinds, that handsome little quail is living in peace and security; and when attacked, it knows that safety lies in running on the ground and not in taking wing and rising clear of the bushes to be shot.

The rigid closing of the markets of New York and Massachusetts against the sale of native wild game has had an immediate and visible effect in rendering wild geese, brant and ducks more plentiful all along the Atlantic coast north of the Carolinas, and also throughout the New England and Middle States. This increase is so marked that once more wild-fowl shooting has become in this part of the world a legitimate sport. The reduction of the four-months' shooting season to three months, as has been done by the federal migratory bird law, will still further promote the return of wild fowl to the northeastern United States, with the prospect that eventually there will be duck-shooting for thousands of sportsmen instead of hundreds only. From October 1 to January 16 you now may go duck-shooting on Great South Bay, and on the bays and lakes of all New England, with a clear conscience; but I repeat that in Connecticut and Rhode Island the sale of game should at once be stopped.

In the state of New York, through the efforts of a really drastic and fairly respected bag-limit law, the ruffed grouse has shown a decided increase in number. I mention it with pleasure as one of the few instances wherein a bag-limit law on birds has accomplished visible results. The bag limit is four birds in one day, or twelve per season. In another five years, that species may become once more sufficiently established that shooting may be resumed, even by conscientious sportsmen. To-day, however, no ruffed grouse should be shot in New York, even though the law offers a margin of four birds per day.

For fifty years, to go no farther back, the American people have been meting out to their quail, pinnated grouse, ruffed grouse, sage-grouse, wild turkey and other upland game-birds a line of treatment that has been *wasteful, improvident, cruel and positively idiotic!* Every person who knows even the rudiments of the habits and mental traits of our upland game-birds knows full well that under real protection all species of them become amazingly tame. By this I mean that after two or three years of genuine immunity from shooting and other forms of molestation, flocks of quail, ruffed grouse, pinnated grouse and even the wild turkey elect to live in cultivated fields and around the barns and stacks of the farmer. I can cite a few

instances of the shy wild turkey, wherein those
naturally wild and timid birds have come into a
protected tract of three hundred acres of cultivated
land, at Deep Lake, sixteen miles east of the settlement of Everglade, on the west coast of Florida,
and are as tame as quails commonly become on
farms where they never are shot at.

*Under a sensible system of conservation, 50,000,-
000 upland game-birds might at this moment be
living on and around the farms, ranches, and other
cultivated lands of the United States, supplying
5,000,000 men and boys with annual hunting and
good food, without one cent of expense to anyone
save the cost of protection from improper slaughter.*

These same birds would devour an annual increment of insects and weed seeds that would mean an
immense additional benefit to the farmers, fruit-
growers and forest-owners of this country.

But for half a century, folly and greed have
marched hand in hand. The people at large who
own the game in general, and the farmers who own
it in particular, have permitted a carnival of
slaughter of upland game-birds that was foolish,
wasteful and wicked. The market-gunners have
been permitted to slaughter the quail and grouse
by the barrel, wagon-load and carload, and ship it to
Chicago, St. Louis and other great markets, to be
sold, or to spoil unsold, as the case might be. A
volume might be written on the wholesale butchery
of American game for the markets, and other forms

of unjustifiable slaughter; but why pursue a subject so painful and humiliating?

What the market-hunters left, the greedy pot-hunters combed out, assisted by sportsmen who believe that it is right to shoot vanishing game just as long as "the *law* permits it!" Now, with the quail and grouse on the point of total disappearance, we come to the next stage of this very exasperating subject.

Having stupidly and criminally permitted the almost-blotting-out of our finest native game-birds, by treatment brutally unfair, the next step of the *un*natural enemies of our wild life was the introduction of foreign species. About fifteen states have attempted to introduce the Hungarian partridge and ring-necked pheasant for the alleged reason that our quail and grouse "can't live" in their own country! Very determined efforts have been made to supplant the bob-white with Hungarian partridges, but I am heartily glad to say that the latter species has been a failure, almost everywhere that it has been tried on a large scale. The very latest confession of failure comes from California. I sincerely hope that the European partridge never will succeed in this country. If the American people are willing that their own quail should be exterminated through greed and folly, I sincerely hope that no foreign species can be found to take its place.

If our quail and grouse are decently treated, and

WILD-FOWL EXTERMINATION ACCORDING TO LAW, BY "PUMP" GUNS

A perfectly legal "bag" of ducks at Kansas City, Mo., shot in March, 1912. An object lesson in spring shooting. The federal migratory bird law now prevents all such bird slaughter in spring.

*sensibly protected, they will come back so rapidly
and so thoroughly that we will not need to look
abroad for substitutes.* But half-way or quarter-
way measures will not serve. They require long
close seasons, and to become effective those close
seasons *must be granted immediately!*

During the past year a fine case of retributive
justice developed in Iowa. The state legislature
was virtually in the act of passing a law to give
Iowa quail a much-needed five-year close season;
but a new and ignorant state game warden elected
to block that legislation, and he successfully did so.
Then, in the plenitude of his wisdom, he undertook
to hatch and rear a great number of pheasants, to
use in stocking the empty covers of the state; and
I am glad to say that his pheasant-breeding operations were a complete failure.

Nevertheless, pheasant raising, which began on
the Pacific coast in 1881, has proven successful in
several states, particularly in Oregon, Washington,
New York and Massachusetts. If the farmers of
the states named had elected to have given to their
quail and grouse the same protection that they
cheerfully accorded the introduced pheasants, those
species would to-day be ten times more abundant
than the pheasants of foreign ancestry.

The transplantation of any wild-animal or wild-
bird species from one country to another is a leap in
the dark. About one-half the efforts made in that
direction have been beneficial, and the other half

have resulted disastrously. Let it be borne in mind
that the introduction of any strange species is
attended with risks, and should not be undertaken
save under expert advice and after the most careful
consideration.

On general principles it is dangerous to meddle
with the laws of nature, and attempt to improve on
the code of the wilderness. Our best wisdom in
such matters may in the end prove to be only short-
sighted folly. The trouble lies in the fact that concerning the transplantation of a species *it is impossible for us to know beforehand all that will affect
it, and all that it will affect.* In its own home a
species may *seem* not only harmless, but actually
beneficial to man. We do not know, and we can
not know, all the influences that keep it in check,
and repress its latent propensities for evil. We do
not know, and we can not know without a trial, how
new environment will affect it, or what new traits
of character it may develop. The gentle dove of
Albion may easily become the tyrant dove of
Cathay. The repressed rabbit of the Old World
becomes in Australia the uncontrollable rabbit, a
devastator and a pest of pests.

It is now against the laws of the United States to
introduce here and acclimatize in a wild state any
wild-bird species without the approval of the
Department of Agriculture. The entry of the Old
World mongoose and the huge fruit-bat known as
the flying fox, is absolutely prohibited. I regard

the flying fox as incapable of injury to the United
States, but the mongoose is a four-footed terror,
to be kept out at all costs. I think that this government could better afford to spend $1,000,000 in
repression than to permit one vigorous pair of
mongoose to become acclimatized in any of our sub-
tropical states. As a destroyer of poultry and
fruit, there is no animal in the American hemi-
sphere that is at all comparable with the vicious and
irrepressible mongoose of the East Indies.

Concerning upland game-birds, we reach the conclusion that for Americans the highest wisdom and
the first duty lies in providing for our own native
species, especially the quail, grouse, ptarmigan and
wild turkey, the protection to which they are justly
entitled, and which, if given, will enable them to
multiply beyond all numbers that reasonably could
be expected of any foreign species. If we protect
our quail properly, we will not need the impossible
Hungarian partridge. If we protect our pinnated
grouse, we will not need the Japanese or English
pheasant. If we wish millions of upland game-
birds for nothing, all we need to do is to give them
the protection that any sane and reasonably intelligent people should be willing and glad to accord.
The great question is, Can the American people
measure up even to a very ordinary standard of
self-repression and self-denial in order to reap
large benefits in the future? The extent to which
the destroyers of our forests are *not* reforesting

offers very small encouragement to the friends of wild life.

There is one subject that I would urge upon the attention of every man who is in any way interested in the development of our existing forests or the creation of new forests. It is the possibilities in the raising of deer in the forests and on the waste lands of the United States.

Without attempting to develop precise figures, let us call to mind the enormous extent of the untillable lands of the United States that are covered with brush and young timber, and also the vast areas of deciduous and coniferous forests. Pause for one moment, and consider the countless square miles of unbroken forest that you have looked upon from your car windows in the East, in the South, in the West, and in southern Canada. Recall the wooded mountains of the Appalachian system, the White Mountains, the pine forests of the Atlantic coast and the Gulf states; the timbered regions of Tennessee, Arkansas and southern Missouri; the scrub-oak belt of Minnesota, and the coniferous forests of every state of the northern Rocky Mountain region. Then think on westward of the silent and untouched forest empire of the Pacific coast, from the Sacramento Valley to Sitka and Mount McKinley. Would ten million deer and elk make any visible impression on that vast green crazy-quilt of forest areas?

But let us, for the moment, confine our thoughts

within the boundaries of the United States. From what we have seen with our own eyes, supplemented by the green areas on the maps that show the existing forests of the United States, I think we are safe in making the estimate that fully one-third of the whole area of the United States is at this moment covered by forests, the remains of forests or brushwood. Moreover, a large proportion of that total area, especially that which is situated in mountainous regions, consists of land that is incapable of cultivation at a profit, and therefore is outside the class of agricultural lands. This being the case, is it not imperative that the American people should seek to make those waste lands produce everything of value that they can produce without prejudice to the development of timber?

Every wild deer that is born in an open forest and rears himself at no expense to the state or to any individual, is a national or state asset of real value. In view of the already enormous cost of beef, pork, mutton and poultry, it is now quite in order to consider our native deer as meat-producing animals and an important source of human food. The logical conclusion regarding land that is utterly unfit for agriculture is that it is available for occupancy by valuable animals, either tame or wild. The grazing of western cattle and sheep in some of the national forests of the Rocky Mountains is already a well-established industry, and wherever it is thoroughly prosecuted there is nothing left for elk and deer.

But there are millions of square miles of other forests in which no herds of cattle and sheep ever will graze, and they seem to remain for deer alone. Imagine for a moment the result of introducing upon all the wild lands of the United States good colonies of deer of the species that is most suitable to them, permitting them to remain for fifteen years unmolested, and then shooting only the young bucks. With the female deer even reasonably well protected, the annual result in pounds of good edible flesh soon would challenge the imagination.

Henceforth, the cost of beef and mutton to the people of this country is bound to remain high. The free grass ranges of Montana, Wyoming and Texas exist no longer on the old basis. Henceforth the great bulk of our beef supply must come, not from the ranches of the cattle kings of the great plains, but from the farms of the middle West; and it will be fattened on corn worth from fifty to sixty cents per bushel. That means high-priced beef. The New York farmer now sells his calves to the butcher because he can not afford to raise them for beef! Odd, is it not? Yet it is quite true.

There are counties in the state of New York, within fifty miles of New York City, that could under adequate management be made to yield annually more pounds of venison than of beef and mutton, and this could be accomplished without the annual expenditure by the state of more than 5 per cent of the value of the venison.

The white-tailed deer is hardy, prolific, a good meat-animal and able to live well in any forest east of the Rocky Mountains. It asks of man nothing save decent protection from indecent slaughter. On the hoof, the adult males weigh from 150 to 300 pounds, according to their position on the map. The smallest members of the white-tailed deer group are those of Florida and the eastern Gulf states, the largest are those on the line from Maine to Michigan, Minnesota, Nebraska, Kansas and Texas.

The unoccupied forest lands of the United States could in my opinion produce annually for our consumption at least 2,000,000 adult deer, without deducting more than $50,000 from the wealth of the nation. Those deer would be worth, at a low estimate, an average of $10 each, which would mean $20,000,000.

By way of illustration let us take the case of Vermont, which is so well fitted to the needs of the moment that it seems to have been specially developed for our use.

In the beginning, the people of Vermont exterminated their original abundant stock of white-tailed deer. In 1870, the species was, so far as known, practically extinct throughout that state. In 1875, a few business men of Rutland decided to make an attempt to restock with deer the open forests around that city. Accordingly they went to the Adirondacks, procured seven female and six male white-tailed deer, took them to a forest six miles from Rutland and set them free.

Those deer took kindly to their new home, persisted and proceeded to stock the state. None were killed, save a few that were shot contrary to law, for twenty-two years.

In 1897, it was decided that Vermont's deer had become sufficiently numerous and well established so that deer-hunting might then begin; but on bucks only. In that year 150 head were killed, and during the next three years, about the same number were taken annually. In 1901, 211 were killed; in 1902, 561; in 1905, 791; in 1907, 1,600; in 1908, 2,208, and in 1909, the grand total was 5,261. For the year last mentioned, 1909, the average weight of the deer killed was 155 pounds each, which for some reason was far below all preceding years, and suggests an error. The total weight of venison taken was 716,358 pounds. Computed at the lowest reasonable valuation, twelve cents per pound, the total value for 1909 would be $85,962.

At this point another factor presents itself for consideration, and that is the damage inflicted by deer upon farm crops. Fortunately for our purpose, Vermont has furnished the answer to that question, even before it is asked.

In Vermont, the deer that now roam all over the state frequently visit farms and gardens and feed upon standing crops. They love peas, beet-tops, turnip-tops, green corn and many other items of the garden. The state of Vermont wisely refrained from the foolish step of shooting deer found damaging crops, but elected that damages should be settled with cash. Furthermore, and for the reason that the counties inhabited by live deer were those that in the hunting season killed and ate of those deer, the state shrewdly decided that each county should pay for the damages inflicted by its own deer. This legislation required the ravaged farmers to pay themselves literally out of their own pockets—a very different proceeding from payment by the state at large, from an impersonal state treasury! Under this system each claim for damages became a neighborhood issue; and for once we have seen claims upon public treasuries kept down to an honest basis.

During the two years 1908 and 1909, the total number of deer claims paid was 311, but the total sum of them was only $4,865. Of those claims, 102 were between $5 and $10 and 80 were under $5. Only four exceeded $100 and the only one which exceeded $200 was the largest claim of all, $326. The total number of deer legally killed during those two years, and not counting several hundred that were killed illegally or by accident, was 7,186, and at $15 per carcass they were worth $107,790 to the people of Vermont. This fairly answers the question whether the payment of those damages was a good investment.

In twenty-two years, from only one small beginning of thirteen head, the state of Vermont produced a valuable annual supply of venison. Against the annual increment must be set a proportion of the cost of state game wardens and the payment of damages, trifling totals, both; and the annual cost of game wardens is usually met by the annual receipts from hunting licenses! Had deer been introduced at a dozen points instead of one only, Vermont could have begun gathering her annual deer crop in fifteen years, instead of twenty-two years. There is no need to wait twenty-two years for the harvest, provided the restocking is done on a reasonably liberal scale.

The people of our country are losing each year an opportunity to produce a large and valuable product in wild flesh food, at practically no cost. Maine is carefully conserving her deer and moose for legitimate shooting by sportsmen. Without counting up the value of the venison annually consumed by the people of Maine, no small item in itself, it is roughly estimated that the non-resident sportsmen who annually go to Maine for deer-shooting add to the wealth of the state at least $1,000,000 per year. This income has been estimated at double the sum we have named; and at all events, the annual deer product in that state is an important state asset. This product is made

possible by sensible game laws, a grasp on the
guides and a real enforcement of the game laws.

Now, what is the great obstacle to the production
of 2,000,000 deer per year in the United States for
food purposes?

Stated without any euphemism, it is the greed,
ignorance and utterly unwarranted notions of
"personal liberty" that often combine in the American individual. The ethics of sport and game preservation in America are as yet in their swaddling
clothes. In fact, it is no exaggeration to say that
until very recently, American sportsmen who shoot
game have been without codes of ethics. With 95
per cent of the men who shoot, the one dominant
idea is to get the game, at all hazards, and in the
killing of it, anything that is "lawful" is necessarily
fair! Millions of game birds and mammals have
been killed in the United States because the law
unwisely permitted it, because the chance offered,
and in order to "kill it before it should be killed by
some other fellow."

Now and then, a faint effort is made toward
giving the game a fair show; but such efforts have
been feeble and spasmodic. Only a few of our
states have emerged from the bogs of barbarism far
enough to protect fawns and female deer, and permit only the killing of bucks with horns not less than
four inches in length. To-day in Pennsylvania a
graduated M.D., backed by a club of alleged
"sportsmen," is bitterly contesting the right of the

state to protect *hornless fawns!* Now, when men of intelligence and means can have the hardihood to defend, even up to the Supreme Court of the state, the killing of a little hornless fawn, what can be expected of the horny-handed and bony-headed backwoodsman who does not dream that there is such a thing as sporting ethics?

The ugly fetich called "personal liberty," which really means license to do as the individual pleases, is the curse of all American wild life and the direct cause of an enormous amount of destruction and local extermination. To-day our vast domains of wooded mountains, hills and valleys lie practically uninhabited by valuable wild life, save in a few exceptional spots that could easily be named. We are losing much because we are so lawless, and because so many of our protective laws are treated as a joke. A law that is foolishly liberal is worse than none. We lose because we are too improvident to conserve our most valuable wild life, unless we are compelled to do so by an officer and a club. We are losing, because our bag-limit laws are a fraud, a delusion and a snare, so far as the real, permanent preservation of game is concerned.

The law-breakers, the game-hogs and the shameless slayers of fawns and does are everywhere. Of all the men in the United States to-day, I believe that fully 10 per cent are already poachers and law-breakers on the sly, or else they are ready to become so to-morrow. The states that contain the greatest areas of wild lands naturally lack in population and in tax funds; and at present, with the national tendencies as they are, not one such state can afford to put into the field even one-half enough salaried wardens to protect her game from surreptitious slaughter. The average frontiersman never admits the divine rights of kings, but he does ardently believe in the divine rights of settlers—to reach out and take any of the products of nature that they happen to need or to fancy.

The dragon that stands between the people of this land and an annual increment of 2,000,000 deer worth $20,000,000 or more, is the *lawless American spirit!* In the dweller on the borders of civilization, and in the backwoods generally, that spirit is hostile to all conservation that restrains the party of the second part from taking what he desires. I now ask the college men of America this question: *Is it possible* to arouse public sentiment in this country to such a pitch of morality, right thinking and right doing, that a rational scheme for raising deer on waste lands, and properly utilizing the increase, can be made possible? If this question were put to me, I would answer that in my opinion such a revolution *is* possible throughout one-half of the territory affected, and even over the other half partial success could be achieved.

The campaign of education and appeal that would be necessary would be tremendous; but in time, when the meat problem becomes more acute than it now is, it will be worth all that it will cost. We lay considerable stress upon this whole matter, because it is the bounden duty of college men to *lead public thought into the right channels,* and not leave ignorant people blindly groping for the truth and the light.

During the past three years, we have seen what great results can be achieved by well-organized campaigns of education and demand. There are certain essentials to the realization of a dream of 2,000,000 deer per year that are imperative; and they are neither obscure nor impossible. The first and the last is a *universal square deal for the deer,* and no killing save in accordance with the rules. The second is that each state and each county proposing to stock its vacant woods with deer must resolutely educate its own people to the vital necessity of playing fair about the killing of deer, and giving every deer and every man fair and just treatment.

If the leading men of each state and county will take this matter seriously in hand, the end that is vitally necessary to success can be attained. The majority of the American people are not insensible to appeals to reason, especially when those appeals are backed up by their own "home folks." Our governors, senators, assemblymen, judges, mayors and justices of the peace could, *if they would,* make a campaign of education and demand that would result in the production of an immense volume of wild food in every state that possesses wild lands.

When the shoe of Necessity pinches hard enough, let the people remember the great possibilities in state and national deer farming. If there can be created for this idea a foundation of sound public sentiment, its success is absolutely assured.

Of course every intelligent person knows full well that the richest and the intensively cultivated farming regions of the United States are not suited to the production and maintenance of wild game of any kind except quail. A state wherein every acre is cultivated, where population is dense and there is a destructive agent on every square rod of earth, is no fit place for grouse, ducks or deer. We do not demand impossibilities. But such regions as I have described are rare. In at least seven-tenths of our states, there is an abundance of woods, swamps and brush-covered hills furnishing suitable cover for quail, grouse and deer. In Massachusetts, Connecticut and New York, where there is an abundance of waste lands, plenty of brush and timber and stone walls instead of barbed-wire fences, the white-tailed deer have enormously increased during the past five years. From the Berkshire Hills they have steadily spread southward until they have reached New York City itself, and the whole north shore of Long Island Sound. I have seen that in Putnam County, New York, the wooded Berkshire Hills and the Croton watersheds are actually becoming populated with deer;

and if the species is given another five-year close season, they will become really numerous.

In this connection it is desirable to set forth pointedly the principle that forms the foundation of our treatment of our almost-vanished species of wild life.

Every wild species of bird or mammal quickly recognizes protection, and takes advantage of it to the utmost.

To the protector of wild life, the most charming trait of wild-life character is the alacrity and confidence with which birds and mammals respond to the friendly advances of human friends. At the present critical stage of our subject, this state of the wild-animal mind constitutes a factor of great importance in arresting the extermination of species and in bringing them back to safe ground. This response to man's protection is manifested not only in harmless quail and song-birds, squirrels, rabbits and beavers, but also in deer, elk, moose, mountain sheep, antelope and grizzly bears.

The tameness of squirrels in city parks is well known. Within the past year, a covey of wild quail has come several times to a rocky ledge within forty feet of our office window in the Zoölogical Park. I have scared gray rabbits off the front door mat of the Administration Building. In December, a gray squirrel entered my office at an open window, evidently seeking new nest-lining materials among the dry scientific pamphlets that

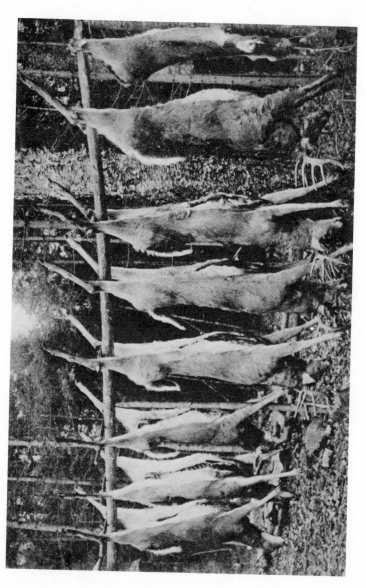

THE WHITE-TAILED DEER AS A FOOD SUPPLY

But the killing of the females was totally wrong.

covered my side-table. In Putnam County, New
York, the deer feed in pastures with the cows and
browse in the gardens. Near Port Jervis, New
York, a ruffed grouse recently nested and hatched
a brood within two feet of the foundation of an
occupied house. In the Wichita Bison Range, in
Oklahoma, many thousand wild ducks now frequent the small stream that runs through it, and
until seen in photographs their masses are unbeliev-
able. At Palm Beach and Tampa, Florida, the
wild ducks know the boundary lines of their protected area quite as well as do any of the gunners.
On their protected waters, they are fearless of man,
but beyond the dead-line they immediately become
wild and wary.

The most conspicuous of all cases of the recogni-
tion of protection by wild animals is to be found
in the Yellowstone Park. This feeling of security is
shared by nearly all the wild animals of the Park,
but it is most strikingly displayed by the herds of
mule deer, antelope and elk that make their home
near Fort Yellowstone and the Mammoth Hot
Springs. In winter the mule deer and antelope are
fed on hay on the parade ground, as if they were
domestic sheep and cattle. At Ouray, Colorado,
bands of mountain sheep pose for photographs at
short range, in the town, in a manner that to every
hunter of that wild and wary species is a profound
surprise.

The bears of the Yellowstone Park also furnish

an amazing exhibition. Everywhere outside the national or state parks, every bear is an Ishmael-ite, on whose head a price is fixed. Knowing well that every man means a rifle and sudden death, the overwhelming impulse of the ursine mind is constantly to watch for his arch-enemy, man, and flee from him the instant he is discovered. In the days of the old-fashioned small-bore muzzle-loading rifle, the grizzly was truculent, aggressive and danger-ous. To-day, a gray rabbit does not turn tail and run away any more quickly or more thoroughly than he. We admire the grizzly for his good sense and his belief in the survival of the fittest; but we do not respect his courage as much as we once did.

The Yellowstone Park grizzlies, and black bears also, are no exceptions to the general influence of peace and protection. Those bears are now famous for the thorough and practical manner in which they have accepted protection, and for years have been reaping the benefits of it. They have become confirmed grafters. They not only make daylight visits to the garbage heaps at the hotels, but they have been known to enter the hotels and walk about in them, looking for offerings of food. Worse than this, they long ago began to raid the cook-tents and mess-wagons of camping parties of tourists, and despoil helpless travelers of hams, sides of bacon and other edibles that are of value in camps. Being unable, by regulation, to shoot any bears in the

Park, even in self-defense, the lot of many a tourist and cook has been rendered decidedly unhappy.

Once, however, the worm did turn. Mr. C. J. Jones, otherwise known as "Buffalo Jones," decided that a certain marauding grizzly had become too great a nuisance to be borne; so after due preparation he roped that grizzly around one of its hind legs, threw the end of the lariat over the limb of a tree, and quickly suspended the bear between the heavens and the earth. While the enraged animal swung in that ignominious position, wildly snapping and clawing at the empty air, Mr. Jones vigorously belabored him with a bean-pole. When the punishment had been well finished, the bear was set free; and instead of pausing to rend the witnesses of his humiliation, or even to punish the author of it, he wildly fled for the tall timber, wherein he turned over a new leaf.

The readiness and the certainty with which wild birds and mammals accept protection, and come back to the old haunts and the old numbers, furnish us with the best of all reasons for providing that protection. It is within the power of the American people to have our country once more teeming with wild life, if the people at large elect to have it so. Within reasonable limits, any partly destroyed wild species can be increased and brought back by giving it absolute protection from harassment and slaughter. This does not mean, however, an annual open season for thirty days, or two weeks, or two days, or any other period. It means *absolute immunity from slaughter* until the stock has become so great that the increase may be taken. Every species that is struggling to recuperate deserves to be left *entirely unmolested,* and free from meddlesome management or alleged assistance in the slaughter of the so-called surplus males. To this well-known law of nature we know of not one exception. Every breeding wild animal craves seclusion, entire immunity from excitement, and protection from all forms of persecution. Nature demands this as her unassailable right.

The methods by which our birds may be encouraged are very simple. First of all, the gunners, netters, dogs and cats must be eliminated. It is now stated by some men who claim to be versed in fox lore that red foxes destroy very little wild bird life. The claim is certainly worthy of serious consideration. In severe winter weather, quail that are struggling to reëstablish themselves should be abundantly fed, and shelters should also be provided. For the perching birds, nest-boxes must be erected, and food offered of kinds suitable to the needs of the various species. For the woodpeckers, nuthatches, chickadees and other special tree-protectors, lumps of suet covered by wire netting, or of fat pork, must be nailed to tree-trunks on the sunny side. The ruffed grouse must sustain themselves, because it is almost impossible to offer them, in a wholesale way, any food that they will accept.

As a final word on the subject of bringing back the birds, I wish to offer a warning against an error. Among the gunners and sportsmen who wish to preserve to the very last their right to kill, we often hear it said that "the cold winters have killed all the quail," and "the cold winters kill more quail than the sportsmen." Now, it is a curious fact that, contrary to all the rules of logic and common sense, the killing of quail by cold winters is by many men advanced as a *reason against better protection for the quail by long close seasons!* It seems incredible that such folly should emanate from reasoning beings; but it does. And, mark you, the men who so mournfully talk about the "cold winters" *never* in the fall refrain from shooting because of a cold winter and decimation. Furthermore, they never advocate five-year close seasons to enable the flocks to recover before being blotted out. No. They heartlessly go right on shooting those half-starved survivors, meanwhile protesting against real protection.

And then, when the end has come, and the covers are tenantless, they seek Hungarian partridges for restocking,—because "our quail can't stand the climate"!

I ask all friends of wild life to insist upon it, in season and out of season, that our quail and grouse *can* stand the climate of their own homes if they are given a square deal and not exterminated by selfish men, dogs and cats. I have no patience with the men who dolefully talk about cold winters and go right on shooting. Let us stand for our native game, right or wrong, and demand for it just and rational treatment. We *can* bring it back if we *will!*

In stocking new game-preserves, both national and private, the question of inbreeding frequently is raised. Naturally, there is solicitude that the original stock should not deteriorate, and private owners usually are willing to expend both effort and money in preventing deterioration through inbreeding.

Several celebrated cases of the inbreeding of wild animals have come to our knowledge, and from them we may draw a definite conclusion. The European red deer of the North Island of New Zealand represents the greatest case of inbreeding of wild animals on record. Originally, New Zealand possessed no large game, and no deer of any kind. In 1864, three European red deer were taken from the royal park at Windsor Castle, England, and after many vicissitudes were liberated not far from Christchurch. The trio consisted of a buck and two does. They found an abundance of food, and promptly they settled down in their new home and began to breed. Now, the North Island contains not less than 10,000 deer, every one of which has descended directly from the famous three. And here is the strangest part of the story: The red deer of New Zealand are to-day physically larger

and more robust, with longer and heavier antlers
and longer hair, than any of the red deer of Europe
west of Germany.   They represent the greatest
inbreeding experiment on record; and the sportsmen of New Zealand have grand sport and take
many fine trophies.

A similar experiment with fallow deer has been
carried out on the island of Lambay, in the Irish
Sea, with three animals transplanted from the
mainland of Ireland in 1892.   From that slender
stock has sprung a large herd, which, but for the
number purposely killed and others that have been
accidentally killed by falling over the cliffs during
storms, now would number several hundred head.
No new blood has been introduced and no deer have
died of disease.   Neither the owner of Lambay, Mr.
Cecil Baring, nor his gamekeepers, have been able
to discover any deterioration in those deer, either in
size, antlers, fertility or general physical stamina.
And yet, strange to say, that island has an area of
only *one square mile,* 640 acres!

These two demonstrations, and others that could
be named, fairly establish the following new
principle:

*When healthy wild animals are established in a
state of nature, either absolutely free, or confined
in preserves so large that they roam at will, seek
the food of nature and take care of themselves, in-
and-in breeding produces no ill effects and ceases to
be a factor.   The animals develop in physical per-*

*fection according to the climate and their food
supply, and the introduction of new blood is not
necessary.*

With domestic animals, full of the diseases of
domestication, inbreeding has a natural tendency
to multiply diseases and accentuate weaknesses.
They breed by artificial selection, they lead lives of
inactivity and their food may or may not be adapted
to their wants. The processes of nature are seriously interfered with, and the domestic animal lives
only because it is strong enough to withstand man's
erratic and faulty treatment. I repeat, therefore,
that with healthy wild animals roaming free in
immense ranges, and seeking nature's food supply,
the evil effects of inbreeding, usually inseparable
from herds of domestic animals, do not appear; and
if the blood of the original stock is good, no new
blood is necessary.

In conclusion, it is quite clear that the business of
bringing back the almost-vanished wild life of our
country, and developing it into an asset of great
value, is a field offering very great possibilities.
Certainly it is worth the serious attention of serious
men. The great obstacles to be overcome are the
ignorance, greed and apathy of a large section of
the public. If they can be overcome, great things
are possible.

CHAPTER IV

ANIMAL PESTS AND THEIR RATIONAL TREATMENT

To any one who attempts to deal with problems and campaigns for the benefit of wild animals, the so-called wild-animal pests quickly become of practical importance. Civilized man is prone to go about with a chip on his shoulder and a gun in his hand, looking for some bird or mammal that has inflicted damage on some of his sacred possessions, in order that he may kill the accused with a conscience most virtuously clear. The loss of a thirty-cent chicken sometimes arouses a twenty-dollar indignation in the breast of a poultry farmer, regardless of a credit balance of perhaps $30 in the hawk's account for rats and mice destroyed.

To know precisely what the real pests *are* among wild mammals and birds seems very much worth while. This knowledge is necessary to the forester, first, in order that he may protect the innocent, and secondly, that the guilty may be brought to justice. Again, there are times in particular localities when the local individuals of a species generally believed harmless, or even valuable, actually may become a nuisance so serious as to require abatement.

In approaching this subject we offer four propositions:

First, A wild bird or mammal species may inflict upon human interests a certain amount of damage, yet not be so destructive as properly to be listed as a pest.

Second, Under exceptional local conditions, a species usually quite harmless may suddenly become so destructive as to compel its classification *locally* as a pest, and to demand its *local* abatement by systematic measures.

Third, Certain species are everywhere so destructive to valuable property that wherever found they should be destroyed.

Fourth, Sometimes destructive individuals are so rare that it is unwise to provide bounties for their destruction, because such bounties often lead unscrupulous or ignorant hunters to destroy valuable birds and mammals, through mistakes in identification, or alleged mistakes.

We can not inveigh too strongly against the ignorant and intolerant spirit that leads a farmer or orchardist to seek revenge upon the bird world for every petty damage that may be inflicted upon his fruit orchard or field crop.

On the other hand, we can not and will not ignore the unbearable damages that sometimes are inflicted by wild birds and mammals on the crops or herds of farmers who can ill afford to submit to a serious waste of the means whereby they live.

On the whole, this subject demands exact knowledge, nice discrimination and judicial treatment. Upon the very threshold of the subject, I wish to impress most strongly upon the mind of every student *the vital necessity of evidence that can stand the test of cross-examination.* It is very desirable that every person who may be called upon to deal with wild life, and decide the fate of creatures that are helpless in their own defense, should spend a few days in a court-room, listening to the trials of half a dozen cases of different kinds. A court-room is the best place in the world in which to learn what constitutes real evidence, and to learn the imperative necessity of taking testimony on both sides of a serious question.

Let me cite a celebrated case bearing on this point, to illustrate what easily becomes the wicked folly of hastily calling a wild species a pest, and condemning it to destruction on insufficient evidence.

For several years prior to the year 1900, the fishermen of San Francisco had been complaining that the sea-lions of the California coast were devouring enormous quantities of salmon and other valuable food fishes, and that they had greatly diminished the annual fish supply. In addition to this, it was claimed that the sea-lions caused great damage to fishermen's nets and impounded fishes. The fishermen formally demanded of the California

State Fish Commission that the sea-lions be destroyed.

Without pausing to make even a pretense of investigating the charges, the Fish Commission ordered that the sea-lions should be destroyed; and the Commission obtained from the United States Light-House Board, in Washington, written permission to carry out the slaughter on the government lighthouse reservations, as well as elsewhere.

The news of the proposed slaughter was at once laid before certain eastern naturalists, who doubted the justice of the death verdict on the sea-lions, and demanded proof that the animals were guilty as charged. Finding that there existed no evidence of a specific and convincing nature, and that no scientific investigation of the food habits of the California sea-lions ever had been made, they entered quick and vigorous protests against the proposed slaughter and demanded its suspension pending an adequate investigation. When the facts in the case were laid before the Light-House Board, the Board's permission to kill was immediately revoked by telegraph.

But the California state authorities had power to act on the water frontage of the state, and in a few localities the killing of sea-lions proceeded.

By good fortune, it happened that during the killing operations that took place in Monterey Bay and vicinity, Prof. L. L. Dyche, of the University of Kansas, arrived upon the scene to pursue special

studies in marine life. Being of an inquiring turn
of mind, he carefully dissected and examined the
stomachs of twenty dead sea-lions that had washed
ashore, and of five others that he killed for the
purpose of mounting their skins. Now mark the
result:

Every stomach examined contained the remains
of squids and devil-fish (*Octopus*), one or both;
both of which are among the fisherman's enemies!
*Not one of the twenty-five stomachs examined con-
tained any portion of a scaled fish!*

In 1901, two investigators from the United
States Fish Commission conducted an extensive
investigation of this subject, and reported upon it
very fully in 1902. At six points on the California
coast they killed twenty-four specimens of the
California sea-lion and eighteen of Stellar's sea-
lion. Their detailed report revealed the fact that
the California sea-lion lives chiefly on squid, and
the diet of the Stellar embraces both squid and
scaled fishes, but as they found it the food of the
latter consisted of an assortment of species of little
value, and contained *not one salmon or shad.*

But for the interference of those meddlesome
eastern naturalists, both the species of sea-lions
inhabiting the coast of California would have been
destroyed, down to a very low point in numbers,
in punishment for crimes of which they were almost
wholly innocent! The obvious moral of this episode
is—*never condemn a wild-animal species on insuffi-*

*cient evidence, and especially not on charges pre-
ferred by ignorant persons.* Investigate; take
testimony on both sides, and be very certain that
you are right before you sign the death warrant.

In taking up our four principles one by one, we
begin with that which concerns the species which
inflict some damage to man's interests, but not
sufficient to deserve death.

A few years ago we heard much about the robins,
blue jays and thrushes that devour cherries and
strawberries and other small fruits. Of late, however, we have heard from the horticulturists very
little on this point. The farmers have learned to
value the good services of those birds, and the birds
themselves have vastly diminished in number. The
agricultural press has rendered such excellent service in behalf of the insectivorous birds that now,
and henceforth, we have little reason to fear that
any American farmer of sufficient industry and
intelligence to maintain fruit-trees will be so ignorant as to kill the insectivorous birds that each season take a few cherries and other small fruits in
payment for their labor in destroying insects.

The most serious indictment against these birds
that I ever have heard comes from the vineyards
along the southern shore of Lake Erie, where the
robin has done serious damage by his habit of
taking a single grape at each descent, thereby for
each grape spoiling the appearance of a marketable
bunch.

The blue jay has been indicted for numerous petty offenses against the farmer, but his record as a destroyer of insects has saved him from punishment. Recently, however, a new fact has been revealed which when fully known should make this saucy and handsome bird the safest from harm of all our small birds. It is known that the eggs of the deadly brown-tail moth hatch in the autumn, and the young pass the winter in nests that are formed in trees. To meet this unusual condition, the blue jay blithely seeks out those nests in winter, tears them open, and devours the contents! Now, if this is not sufficient to induce every forester to look upon the blue jay with a protecting eye, nothing ever will avail.

Various species of blackbirds destroy small amounts of grain, but I never knew a farmer to kill one on that account. No one else knows half so well as the plowman the industry and success of our old friend the purple grackle in gleaning the abominable white grub-worms out of the freshly turned furrows, and the lonesome plowman finds real companionship in the birds that follow him with cheerful industry, hour after hour, when the field is destitute of other company.

Only once have I ever known an individual crow to be so diligent in wrong-doing as to deserve the death penalty. In 1902, many young ducks were hatched in the Zoölogical Park, and no sooner had the ducklings taken to the waters of the Wild-

Fowl Pond than they attracted the deadly attention of an old crow, also nesting in the Park, with a
nestful of young of her own to maintain. She
began feeding those ducklings to her brood, and her
industry soon became appalling. After the sixth
duckling had been swept into that corvine vortex, it
became painfully evident that we must choose
between one brood of crows and about one hundred
ducklings. It became our painful duty to order
the destruction of that crow; which was done; and
her nestlings were taken and reared by hand. That
was the first and last occasion on which we
ever found it necessary to sign a death warrant
returnable against a crow. Crows may easily be
kept out of a cornfield by erecting a scarecrow
representing a *man with a gun.*

Concerning the fruit-eating habits of a number
of our most valuable insectivorous birds, there is
one way out of the difficulty that is obvious, but
very, very rarely carried into effect. It consists
in the planting of a few Russian mulberry and
sweet-cherry trees on every farm, especially for the
birds. For four years, State Game Commissioner
John M. Phillips, of Pittsburgh, has been educating the people of Carrick, Pennsylvania, old and
young, into this method of attracting birds, and
providing for their needs. The fruit of the Russian
mulberry is greatly liked by birds, and it ripens
continuously throughout four months of the year.

There should be inaugurated a general movement for the planting of these trees.

Our second subject relates to the species of birds and mammals that *usually* are harmless, but under exceptional local conditions sometimes become pests that require abatement.[1]

The principle involved is best explained by examples. The most world-famous case is that of the introduction of the European rabbit in Australia. Under the restrictions imposed by hunters, poachers, hawks and owls in densely populated England, the English hare is so scarce as to be harmless. In Australia, with abundant food, a hospitable climate and practically nothing to keep the species in check, it multiplied to such an extent as to constitute an intolerable pest. In southern California, Texas and Oklahoma, the wild jack-rabbit in the same manner once increased so enormously that wholesale killing measures became necessary to keep down the total.

In one locality in the state of Oregon, eagles once became so numerous that their depredations on the lambs of the flocks of the sheep-owners became too great to be borne. When the case was laid before

[1] The crow has long been fought over, by a small minority that recounts his wrong-doings and demands his blood, which is opposed by an overwhelming majority that recounts the bird's good deeds and resolutely prevents his being slaughtered. It is perfectly true that some of the ways of the crow are very trying; but when all the evidence has been brought in and weighed and measured, the good deeds of the crow in devouring grasshoppers, cutworms and other bad insects, meadow mice and other bad rodents, are so many that *Corvus* seldom is condemned to wholesale destruction.

an eastern bird protector and his judgment was asked, he advised that the over-supply of eagles should by shooting be reduced to a point sufficiently low so that subsequent depredations would be endurable. Fortunately, that condition was confined to a small area and it was by no means necessary to enact a general law providing for state-wide eagle destruction. In fact, such a law would have been a mistake.

About five years ago a gentleman living on Shelter Island, near the eastern end of Long Island, liberated a herd of white-tailed deer in a county wherein deer-shooting is permitted by law on two days only of each year. Two years later, complaints were made that on Shelter Island it was impossible to maintain a vegetable garden, on account of the depredations of deer. It was claimed that it was impossible to build a wire fence high enough so that those deer could not leap over it; but that statement was, and is, open to doubt. The conditions described above suggested a law to provide for the abatement of wild-animal nuisances, which was proposed by the framers of the revised game-laws of the state of New York, and adopted. It appears in the code of that state as Section 158, and its full text is as follows:

Power to Take Birds and Quadrupeds. In the event that any species of birds protected by the provisions of section two hundred and nineteen of this article, or quadrupeds protected by law, shall at any time, in any locality, become destructive

of private or public property, the commission shall have power
in its discretion to direct any game protector, or issue a permit
to any citizen of the state, to take such species of birds or
quadrupeds and dispose of the same in such manner as the
commission may provide. Such permit shall expire within four
months after the date of issuance.

We commend this measure for enactment into
law in every state of the Union, on the ground that
it offers a rational and safe remedy for many
legitimate grievances that otherwise can not be
redressed. There is no reason why wild animals
should be permitted to destroy large quantities of
private property without recourse.

In a previous lecture we referred with some detail
to the damages of wild deer to the gardens, orchards
and farm crops of Vermont, and the Vermont
treatment of such cases. Each county is authorized
and required to settle in cash the damages inflicted
upon its own residents, and the system is in operation throughout the state, apparently to the satisfaction of every one concerned. It having been
reported that female deer, hitherto immune from
slaughter, had become so numerous and so tame
that they constituted a nuisance, the state very
wisely and justly decided that it was necessary to
reduce the number. Accordingly, a law was passed
permitting the killing of female deer, with the
intent to leave it in force until the total number of
female deer has been reduced to a proper point,
when it will be repealed.

In small city parks, gray squirrels can easily become so numerous as to constitute a pest to nesting birds. It is a mistake to permit one hundred squirrels to exist in a park so small that it has room for only twenty or less. A swarm of restless and hungry squirrels will attack nesting birds, and devour both eggs and young birds. A park that has become infested with red squirrels—our most destructive and objectionable species—deserves to be delivered from the pest by the use of a .22-caliber rifle, fitted with a Maxim silencer in order that the process may not be made painfully conspicuous in the ears and eyes of the public.

I am distinctly not in favor of slaughtering birds merely because at rare intervals they flock in grain-fields and consume grain. The period wherein grain destruction is possible is *very brief;* and the proper way to protect the crops is by spending a few dollars in systematically frightening the birds and compelling them to move on. In all such cases, the shot-gun should be the farmer's last resort, not the first. I am a firm believer in the use of blank cartridges in the preservation of fruit and field crops from the unbearable attacks of birds, but the farmer who uses them runs the risk of being without his feathered friends when he most needs their aid!

The time was, a few years ago, when we all conceded that the rice-growers of the Carolinas had a moral right to hire negroes to slaughter bobolinks (or rice-birds) with shot-guns, for the protection of the rice crops. To-day the rice-growing industry in the Carolinas is nearly dead, and the old conditions no longer exist. There now remains no excuse whatever for the slaughter of bobolinks for sport, for food or to protect crops. The bobolink-ricebird is no longer in the pest class, and it deserves the same permanent protection that is accorded the robin and thrush.

The bobolink is a useful bird; but mark you the ill turn it has been served by the evil reputation that forty years ago was forced upon it by the rice planters of the Carolinas. Because it ate rice, that beautiful songster, which part of the year does good execution on insects and weed seeds, was shot for food, as an alleged "pest." Sportsmen entered into the slaughter and some have continued in it. By reason of this ancient, out-of-date and now wholly libelous excuse, the sportsmen of certain states now continue to shoot bobolinks as "game." Strangest of all bird-killing spectacles, every autumn we see in the District of Columbia, about 1,100 gunners take the field, and slaughter bobolinks for "sport," all around the Capitol of this bird-protecting nation!

Everywhere throughout the world, save in one place, the killing of female hoofed and horned game is, by conscientious men and true sportsmen, regarded as highly destructive to species, and therefore quite inadmissible. No species can long withstand the destruction of its mothers! No man who kills female hoofed game for sport can properly be called a sportsman, nor can he be said to have a code of ethics. But there is one exception to this otherwise universal rule regarding female hoofed game, and I mention it because of the very great rarity of such cases. It relates to the elk of the Yellowstone Park.

For many years past, the finest and largest male elk of the Yellowstone Park herds have been shot to death outside the Park by sportsmen and poachers, for their heads and "tusks." As a result of this relentless culling-out process, it is now very difficult to find in Wyoming or Montana a large bull elk with a really heavy and imposing pair of antlers. The twelve-point bulls are not only very few in number, but their antlers are, as a rule, light and mediocre. And yet, the actual number of elk in the Yellowstone region is 47,000; and only recently there was great elk starvation in the Jackson Valley, the winter home of the great park herds.

As an actual fact, there is at present a great oversupply of *female* elk and an alarming insufficiency of winter grazing-grounds. In addition to these evils, the sires of the great elk herds are *immature animals,* really unfit for breeding purposes; and their calves, many of them, are too weak to survive their first winter.

This situation is beset with problems and difficulties. Our own answer to the puzzle is that *the stock of breeding females must resolutely be reduced, and the sires of the herds must be improved.* Our advice is: For five years stop the killing of *male* elk, and during that period kill 2,500 *cow* elk each year. This plan we believe is the only solution of the elk problem that ever will prove effective, and place the herds on a firm basis for the future.

A few years ago, certain interests in Pennsylvania raised a great public outcry against the alleged awful destruction of fish in the streams of Pennsylvania by herons. The case was made so serious that the fish commissioner demanded that state protection be removed from the herons and certain other birds. The state game commissioners were hoodwinked into accepting the charges as true, and they virtually permitted the throwing of the herons into the arena of slaughter. A little later on, however, the game commissioners found that the herons remaining in Pennsylvania were far too few to constitute a pest to fish life, and furthermore, the millinery interests appeared to be behind the movement. Under the new law the milliners were enabled *to reopen in Pennsylvania the sale of aigrettes,* because those feathers came from members of the unprotected Heron Family! It required a tremendous state campaign to restore protection to the herons and bar out the aigrettes; but it was accomplished in 1912.

Hereafter, let no man for one moment be deceived by the claim that the very few-and-far-between herons, bitterns and kingfishers that now remain in the United States, anywhere, are such a menace to fish life that those birds are a pest and deserve to be shot. The inland streams of the United States and Canada lack fishes because they have been outrageously overfished,—wastefully, wickedly depleted, without sense or reason, by men who scorn the idea of conservation. In Orleans County, New York, a case was reported to me of a farmer who dynamited the waters of his *own creek, in spawning time!*

Go where you will, wherever fish still exist in our interior waters, and you will not be long in hearing stories of fish slaughter and fish waste that will amaze and anger you. In view of all the wickedness that has been perpetrated on the game-fishes of our fresh-water streams and ponds, I have no patience with any of the stories of great fish slaughter by herons, kingfishers or any other wild birds. Such stories deserve the contempt of everyone who hears them. At this moment, after fifty years of wasteful and wicked fish destruction, the great and virtuous state of Texas is about to condemn to death the remaining pelicans of her gulf coast—because they eat fish! Even a state can be both stupid and mean, the same as an individual; and to charge to wild birds the fish extermination that has been perpetrated by man is both false and cowardly.

Before we leave this section of our subject, I wish to add a pointed word of warning.

There are very many confirmed destroyers of wild life who lose no opportunity to charge up to other causes the evil results of their own practices. For example, the relentless quail-killer will look you squarely in the face, and with never a blush mantling his cheek, he will tell you "the hard winters kill more quail than sportsmen do." The squirrel-shooter will declare that birds are scarce because the squirrels rob their nests and eat their young; and this in a region where now there is only one wild squirrel to every ten square miles.

Do not accept seriously any fantastic statement or theory regarding alleged great damages that have been inflicted upon valuable interests by wild birds or mammals, until indisputable evidence has been laid before you. Out in Arizona, the desert men say, "Snake stories don't go unless you produce the rattles." With us stories of havoc and destruction by "pest" birds and "pest" mammals "don't go" unless we can see good proof. During our late unpleasantness in Congress with the feather millinery trade (1913), our opponents very strenuously insisted upon their right to import the feathers and skins of birds that had been killed as "pests." We met that claim, and vanquished it, by demanding to be shown any country in the world that sends forth a noteworthy *commercial feather product* from birds that have been killed solely *because* they were pests, and irrespective of the feather millinery trade. We demanded to be shown a commercial product, from any source, of genuine "pest" bird feathers. Nothing of the kind could either be shown or described. The hawk, eagle and condor feathers that enter the feather markets of Europe come from birds that are sought out and killed *especially for the feather trade.*

The first reply to make to every demand for the destruction of wild bird and mammal pests is this: "Show me the *proof!* Give me facts that would be regarded as *evidence in a court of law;* then I will believe it, but not before."

We now come to our third proposition, which embraces the wild species that everywhere are so destructive to valuable property that they deserve to be destroyed, and concerning which there is no dispute.

At the head of this list of evil-doers stands the big *Gray Wolf or "Timber" Wolf,* strong of limb and jaw, insatiable in appetite, a master of cunning and the acme of cruelty. The states that still possess gray wolves have done well in placing a high cash bounty, varying from $10 to $25 on the head of this four-footed fiend. At this moment, many a forest ranger west of the great plains is on the alert for signs that will show the location of the dens of breeding pairs of gray wolves, in order that if possible the parents may be destroyed before the young are born; or, failing that, that the young may be destroyed in the spring before they leave the den.

Ever since the range steer took the place of the American bison, a relentless warfare has been waged against the gray wolf. The hordes of gray marauders that once battened and fattened on the millions of wasted buffalo carcasses have been reduced to scattered fragments. On the plains there is to-day perhaps one gray wolf to every hundred that were there prior to 1885. The cowboy and the professional wolfer have enormously reduced the wolf population; but for all that, it seems impossible to exterminate the species, or even to prevent the continuous slaughter of stock. The doubled values of cattle and sheep have led to increased activities in the destruction of wolves, but at the same time it has intensified the keen ability of the wolf to preserve his own life under most adverse circumstances.

The intelligence of the gray wolf in securing his prey, and in avoiding traps, poison, dogs and firearms, is unsurpassed in anything of flesh and blood. The disappearance of the wild game throws the subsistence of the wolf-pack upon the ranchman and stock-owner. Thanks to the bounty system, the total number of wolves now alive in the United States is small. In 1912, the rangers of the United States Forestry Bureau killed 241 gray wolves, and during a similar period the Province of British Columbia alone accounted for 518 wolves.

The gray-wolf area embraces about three-fourths of the entire continent of North America, and it includes the entire Rocky Mountain region of the United States and the Sierra Madre of Mexico down to Guadalajara. Wherever found, the proper course with a wild gray wolf is to kill it as quickly as possible. While it is quite possible to catch gray wolves in steel traps, success in such endeavors is very difficult to attain. Poison is the best exterminator, but its successful use calls for expert knowledge. The best of all methods is to destroy the young in their dens, as soon as possible after their birth. The destructiveness of the gray wolf is concentrated on the young of range stock, colts, calves, half-grown cattle and sheep being the principal victims. Of wild game, the deer and antelope are the greatest sufferers, and to both those species the gray wolf is terribly destructive.

In regions that now are almost destitute of game, the gray wolf, when hard pressed by hunger, sometimes becomes deadly dangerous to man. It has been stated that there is not on record in America one well-authenticated instance of a human being having been attacked and killed by gray wolves. Now, however, there are two such cases on record, and we believe that the evidence on which they rest is true. It is reported that near the close of 1912, a mail-carrier serving the lumber-camps above Lake Nipigon, about sixty miles north of Lake Superior, in the Province of Ontario, was killed and completely devoured by wolves. Four large wolves were killed by the carrier before he was overpowered. This is said to have been the second occurrence of that kind in that region, and a reign of terror was the result!

Everything that has been said regarding the gray wolf may be repeated regarding the *Coyote,* but in a decidedly minor key. The latter is smaller and weaker, cowardly instead of courageous, inferior in cunning, and even though far more numerous, its depredations are less serious. The specialty of this animal is deer and antelope fawns, grouse and quail. In the United States its range is generally the same as that of the gray wolf. While the United States forest rangers were destroying 241 gray wolves in 1912, they killed 6,478 coyotes, and in the same period British Columbia accounted for 3,563.

The good services performed by the coyote consists in the destruction of prairie-dogs, Franklin spermophiles and other burrowing rodents that are injurious to land and crops. These services, however, are completely overshadowed by the slaughter of young calves, colts and lambs. The pronghorned antelope often falls a victim to this pest. The coyote is an Ishmaelite. Every man's hand is against him and he should be killed wherever found in a wild state.

The *Mountain Lion* of the West, known to us as the puma or cougar, also is a destructive, dangerous

and intolerable pest. Wherever it is numerous it is
fearfully destructive to deer and young elk, and it
must be hunted down and destroyed regardless of
cost. In California the annual slaughter of deer by
pumas is said to be enormous. It is the deadliest
enemy of the big game of every region which it
inhabits. It kills mountain sheep, elk, deer, and
every other species of game of attractive size that
lives within its haunts. In the Yellowstone Park
so many elk calves were killed by pumas it became
necessary for Mr. C. J. Jones to procure a pack of
dogs and regularly exterminate as many pumas as
could be found. Around the entrance of one puma
den the hunters found the skulls of nine elk calves.
During that campaign a large number of pumas
were hunted down and killed; but for all that, the
number still remaining in the Yellowstone Park is
estimated by the Park officers at 100. In 1912
our forest rangers killed 88 pumas, and British
Columbia destroyed 277.

The disappearance of wild game, and the spread
of stock-raising into the home of the *Grizzly* and
Black Bear of the West, very naturally has led to
the destruction of range cattle by bears, to an
unbearable extent. It is now a well-known fact
that if bears are left unmolested and permitted to
become numerous, they quickly acquire the idea
that they are immune and grow bold accordingly.
On such a basis, stock-killing is a quick and sure
result. While we are unalterably opposed to the

extermination of species, we believe that dangerous and destructive predatory animals must be shot down to a point sufficiently low so that they are no longer a nuisance that stalks abroad at noonday. One grizzly on every one hundred square miles of Rocky Mountain territory is sufficient to impart a distinctly ursine flavor to the wilderness and maintain the charm that is best expressed by the term "wild country."

In the Yellowstone Park, the grizzly bears have become so numerous and aggressive it has been necessary, for the safety of the public, to reduce the number. This has been done, not by shooting the surplus, but by capturing the most offensive animals alive and unhurt, in steel cages, and shipping them to zoölogical gardens and parks. We are unalterably opposed to the capture of the American king of beasts in steel traps, and subjecting him to a sordid and ignominious death. For him, any other death than by a sportsman's rifle, after a fair stalk, is unacceptable. Trapping bears, either to destroy them as pests or to kill them for their fur, never should be tolerated in any civilized country. If wild bears become so numerous as to constitute a menace to public safety, a scourge to private property and a genuine pest, then let that fact be made known in the press, and let sportsmen be invited to come in and reduce the ursine population. Of course there is no objection to a forest ranger hunting down and shooting an objectionable bear, but we strongly object to steel traps and poison. It happens, however, that the great American sportsman has so thoroughly done his work in grizzly-bear slaughter that to-day it is almost an impossibility for a tenderfoot sportsman to find an unkilled grizzly in any hunting-ground within the borders of the United States. When inquirers ask, "Where can I go and kill a grizzly in this country?" the reply is, "Nowhere!"

The *Lynxes,* wherever found, are a pest, though not in the class of great pests. Their depredations correspond to their size, and are confined chiefly to game-birds and small game-quadrupeds. The rabbit family is the mainstay of the lynx, and when rabbits fail, the lynxes are quickly reduced to a state bordering upon starvation. Although it is known that a lynx can and occasionally does kill a mountain sheep, such occurrences are, we believe, extremely rare. An undue abundance of lynxes soon could become an intolerable nuisance, but owing to the rarity of lynxes as they are found at this time, they are almost a negligible factor.

In farming communities, the *Mink, Weasel, Skunk, Raccoon,* and even the *Opossum,* all become so destructive to poultry as to constitute pests that require to be suppressed. I have in my possession a photograph showing the remains of twenty English pheasants that were killed by one weasel in one night. Every individual of the five species named—mink, skunk, raccoon, opossum and weasel—is to be regarded as a perpetual enemy of poultry and, unless extenuating circumstances can be found, deserves death. It follows most naturally that a savage little beast which by disposition and weapons is fitted to destroy all kinds of poultry will, in wild regions, be equally destructive to valuable bird life, especially those species that live on or near the ground.

Regarding the *Red Fox* and his relatives, there is an unsettled dispute. For many years this species has occupied a place in the class of pests, and on that basis his pelt has been demanded. Quite recently, in the columns of a sportsman's magazine, defenders of the fox have arisen, who stoutly declare that to their positive knowledge, based on many years' experience, the red fox is *not* a great destroyer of game-birds and poultry, as has been charged in the indictments against him. Certain it is that grouse and quail, and other ground-nesting birds, never were so numerous as in the days when the foxes of the United States were most numerous. It would almost seem as if it is the way of the fox to live upon the lame, the halt and the blind among upland game-birds, and by catching and consuming the weakest to promote the survival of the fittest. It is quite certain, however, that foxes are very destructive to woodland grouse in winter, when the latter are heavily handicapped by deep snow.

For the game of North America, large and small, it has been a fortunate thing that the destruction and disappearance of the fur-bearing animals—game-killers nearly all of them—has fully kept pace with the general destruction of game. In view of the destruction of the wild food supply, it is not strange that to-day the wolves, coyotes, pumas and bears are compelled to resort to the cattle, sheep, horses, pigs and poultry of the farmer and ranchman in order to avoid starvation.

The birds that now are known to be more destructive than beneficial are few in number, but fairly conspicuous. Few indeed are the birds of North America whose depredations are so pronounced and so constant that they create a general average of wickedness that is intolerable and clearly deserving of death. It is a serious matter to condemn a species to death by violence, and American naturalists have learned the wisdom of not signing death warrants hastily or on insufficient evidence. After all has been said, there appear to be only seven bird species so totally depraved, and so unprotected by mitigating circumstances, that the verdict of guilty is unanimous.

The *Sharp-Shinned Hawk,* a near relative of the falcons, is a keen hunter, a swift flyer and a relentless murderer of small birds. In size it is next to our pigeon-hawk and third from the sparrow-hawk, the smallest of all. It hunts along fences and hedges like a dog hunting rabbits, and pursues songbirds into and through their thickets like a winged mongoose. Its principal food is song-birds, and rarely does it capture a mouse. It is rather too small to handle domestic poultry with complete success, but it can be very destructive to young pheasants and quail.

A complete list of the contents of 159 sharp-shinned hawk stomachs reveals a tale of slaughtered innocents that is appalling. Ninety-nine contained song-birds, woodpeckers, etc., 6 contained poultry, 6 contained mice, 5 contained insects and 52 were empty. All North America, north of Guatemala, constitutes the breeding-ground and hunting-ground of the sharp-shin, and wherever found, old or young, it should be killed without compunction.

Cooper's Hawk is the companion in crime of the preceding species, and equally deserving of an early and violent death. In form and color it bears a strong resemblance to the sharp-shin, but it is a much larger bird. Being a bird of strong and rapid flight, much strength and activity and also great boldness, it is well equipped for raiding poultry-yards and pheasant-farms, and carrying off almost everything except geese, turkeys and large ducks. Of 133 stomachs examined, 34 contained poultry or game-birds, 52 contained other birds, 11 contained small mammals, 1 contained a frog, 3 contained lizards, 2 contained insects, and 39 were empty. The game-bird species consisted of 1 ruffed grouse, 8 quail and 5 pigeons. Altogether, 21 species of useful birds had been eaten and only 4 mice, 1 rat and 1 grasshopper. No bird record could be much blacker than this. The Cooper's hawk, which inhabits the whole United States, is an unqualified pest, deserving of swift and sure destruction.

The *American Goshawk,* chiefly confined to Canada and Alaska, is a wholesale destroyer of game-birds, serves no useful purpose, and deserves destruction. Fortunately, it is nowhere numerous and is rarely seen.

The *Duck-Hawk* or *Peregrine Falcon,* inhabiting all America north of Chili, is another hated destroyer of game-birds and song-birds, with no extenuating circumstances save at very long intervals a lonesome mouse or insect. Each bird of this species deserves treatment with a choke-bore gun. First shoot the male and female, then collect the nest, the young or the eggs, whichever may be present. They all look best in collections.

The *Pigeon-Hawk,* second from the smallest species of our hawks, is fearfully destructive to our best beloved song-birds. It kills thrushes, goldfinches, vireos, bobolinks, sparrows, swifts and many other species. Kill it without mercy! Out of 56 specimens examined, 41 contained song-birds. In shooting this dull-gray bird, be careful not to kill the beautiful little sparrow-hawk—dull blue, bright rusty brown, white, black and salmon color—because it is a phenomenal destroyer of insects. The sparrow-hawk is probably the most valuable of all our hawks, and also the most beautiful.

The time was when we could hesitate before deciding the fate of the *Great Horned Owl,* but owing to the enormous decrease in bird life that period has gone by. To-day the horned owl is an aërial murderer and robber, and the benefits he confers in rat-killing are completely buried under a mass of slaughtered song-birds, ruffed grouse, quail, pigeons, ducks and other birds. I advise every forest ranger to kill every great horned owl that he can kill, and thereby save hosts of useful birds. In British Columbia the great horned owl has been, and still is, a great scourge to the upland game-birds—grouse, ptarmigan and quail. The game-birds were so abundant that presently the owls became epicurean in their tastes and often ate only the brains of their prey. Then systematic warfare began, and in two years, 1910 and 1911, 3,139 great horned owls were killed. The provincial game warden, Mr. A. Bryan Williams, declared in his last annual report that since the destruction of those owls the grouse had visibly increased.

The rather small and slender *Long-Eared Owl* should live. He destroys a few sparrows, but these are paid for three times over by his slaughter of wild mice of many species. Of all owls he is the greatest mouser.

The *Short-Eared Owl* is in all respects an understudy of the long-eared, and deserves similar immunity from slaughter, and protection.

The *Barred Owl* is as omnivorous as the raccoon.

He not only eats mice and other small rodents, frogs, lizards, fishes, crawfish, a few sparrows and other small birds, but he cheerfully and impartially takes in every screech-owl and saw-whet owl that he can catch. It is the only owl known to us that can frighten small birds in an aviary, induce them to dash against the wire netting and actually seize and devour them through netting of one-inch mesh. The barred owl should be killed, because it is a pest.

Beyond question, throughout the Rocky Mountain region, the *Golden Eagle* is a great pest to certain species of large game. The destruction of mountain sheep lambs, antelope fawns and mountain goat kids by this bird is quite serious. For this reason, and others, in British Columbia the golden eagle is officially regarded as a pest, and its numbers have been systematically reduced. In 1910 and 1911, 102 golden eagles were killed in that province, as I believe with entire justice.

The transactions of British Columbia in destroying wild animal pests afford an interesting and instructive exhibit. During two years' operations, 1910 and 1911, there were destroyed a total of 2,896 gray wolves and pumas and 5,141 coyotes, in addition to the horned owls and golden eagles already noted. Allowing fifty head of game to each gray wolf and to each puma, and ten to each coyote (very fair estimates, we think), the total number of game and domestic animals *saved* each year by the killing of those marauders would amount to 191,210 head. I think that an estimate of one victim per week for each adult puma and gray wolf is not extravagant.

In California there is made the same killing estimate for the puma, fifty victims per year. If this is anywhere near correct, then the one hundred pumas estimated among the wild animals present in the Yellowstone Park must devour nearly 5,000 head of game each year.

The extermination of wild-animal pests in national, state and private forests is a large subject. It is beset with difficulties and perplexities. Owing to the frailty of human nature when it carries a gun, the Forest Service of the nation and the state is deprived of a valuable line of outside assistance to which by all rights it is entitled. Outside assistance in shooting pest animals often is more deadly than the pests themselves. The one thing that a man with a gun finds it hardest to resist is temptation; temptation to shoot everything that might, could, would or should be a "pest" mammal or bird. Whenever an unscientific gunner takes the field to shoot "pest" hawks, it is time for all hawks to take to the tall timber. The assembly of erroneous heads that were sent in to Harrisburg for bounties during the prevalence of the "fool hawk law" is an ancient but still living joke in the Pennsylvania State Game Commission.

Remembering this, the Commission is now sorely perplexed by the prospect that offers of fresh bounties for the destruction of "vermin" will lead to the slaughter of a great number of quadrupeds and birds under cover of the law, by alleged mistakes in identification. The secretary of the Commission has sent broadcast a stern warning to the effect that no mistakes in the hunting of pests will be tolerated.

The gray wolf has been pursued with great vigor and vengefulness, and although an enormous number has been killed, the supply seems inexhaustible. At times, "Old Lobo" drives a ranchman to despair. In all-around cunning and resourcefulness, bears and pumas are mere amateurs in comparison. There is no royal road to any gray-wolf pelt, but a $25 bounty is certain to reduce the wolf population very effectively. A few years ago, a gathering of stock-growers convened in Seattle to meet an expert who had been invited and urged to come over into Macedonia and instruct the populace on the latest methods of wolf destruction. The assembly rashly concluded that it was about to receive a sovereign remedy, a genuine specific for the cure of stock-slaughter.

When all had been said by the stock-men, the government expert announced that the best way to destroy wolves was to locate the dens and then destroy both old and young. The proletariat was greatly disappointed. It had expected a quick and sure remedy, and it laughed the expert to scorn. But the mistake was its own. There never was any reason for the belief that human intelligence could devise a sure and certain method for finding and killing the most cunning and capable of all American predatory animals except the wolverine.

The eradication of the puma from certain districts that it now infests to a deplorable extent is a task of immediate urgency, and it should not be lost to view because of the wolf question. At this moment pumas are a curse to the deer, elk and other game of the Yellowstone Park, the Kaibab Plateau, on the western rim of the great Colorado Canyon, and in southern and southeastern California. The puma is very successfully hunted with dogs that have been trained to trail it, and this is legitimate sport in which outsiders may engage with safety to the other game. Once popularize it, and the doom of the puma is sealed. For all wild-animal pests (except bears) that kill fifty deer or elk calves per capita each year, we consider fire-arms, dogs, traps and strychnine thoroughly legitimate weapons of destruction. For such animals, no half-way measures will suffice.

The *rabbit plague* in New Zealand and Australia, already mentioned, is so well known as to require little comment. It is a useful illustration of what a seemingly harmless animal can do when circumstances enable it to live and breed without restraint. The introduction of the rabbit into Australia was deliberately done, to furnish sport and an additional food supply.

"The inhabitants of Australia," says Dr. Lydekker, "soon found that the rabbits were a plague, for they devoured the grass, which was needed for the sheep, the bark of the trees and every kind of fruit and vegetable, until the prospects of the colony became a very serious matter, and ruin seemed inevitable. From New South Wales upwards of 15,000,000 rabbit skins have been exported in a single year, while in thirteen years ending with 1889, no less than 39,000,000 were accounted for in Victoria alone.

"To prevent the increase of these rodents, the introduction of weasels, stoats, mongooses, etc., has been tried; but those carnivores neglected the rabbits and took to feeding on poultry, and thus became as great a nuisance as the rabbits themselves. An attempt to kill the rabbits by an epidemic disease also failed. Wire fences, sometimes 150 miles long, have been erected to bar rabbits from new territory."

In New Zealand the increase of rabbits in twenty years has been so enormous that in some districts it has become a question whether the colonists should not vacate the country rather than attempt to fight the plague. But the fur trade now raises the star of hope in Australia. Rabbit fur is now in so great demand that about twenty million rabbit skins are annually exported from that continent to Europe. Rabbit fur is now dyed and sold by furriers under the following trade names: seal, electric seal, Hudson seal, Red River seal, sable, French sable, sable coney and seal coney.

Occasionally during the past twenty years, jack-rabbits so greatly increased in Colorado and southern California that great rabbit drives became necessary, in which the rabbits were destroyed by wholesale methods.

Unhappy Australia is now struggling with a new pest. About thirty years ago, the European red fox was introduced, to establish the noble pastime of fox hunting; and the result was an escape of foxes that soon began to stock the country. Having no natural enemies to contend with except man, the foxes soon found themselves in a vulpine paradise. They are industriously devouring all kinds of wild mammals and birds except the largest species, domestic poultry, pigs and lambs, and it is believed that they will eventually spread all over Australia. The government offers a bounty on fox scalps, but the increase of the pest continues.

In America the English sparrow is now a national sorrow. This pest is past eradication, save by an effort so great and so costly that no such effort *ever* will be put forth. All Americans declare with irritation that "the English sparrow is a nuisance, and ought to be exterminated"; but there the matter rests.

And now comes the European starling, a short, thick bird of black plumage strongly penciled with light-colored streaks, a yellowish beak and a cheery whistle. It flocks around man's habitations, swarms in his parks and remains all winter. In the breeding season it routs the woodpeckers, bluebirds, purple martins and other good and desirable birds out of the nest-boxes that have been erected especially for them, and takes possession. A flock of starlings can easily dispossess and drive away golden-winged peckers, and have been seen to do so. Fortunately, the starling is not a street-gutter scavenger, like the English sparrow; but if it continues to drive away our woodpeckers and other native birds, as it now seems to be doing, its extermination will be very much in order.

There is one foreign wild-animal pest that is continually knocking at our doors, and whenever it obtains a foothold, its presence will spell calamity. It is the *Mongoose;* a small carnivorous mammal about as large as a large mink, which finds it home in India, Ceylon, Burma and other countries of the Orient. Although an animal of small size, its restless energy, fierce temper, indomitable courage and physical activity enable it to vanquish birds and some mammals of ten times its own size.

In its home country, India, the mongoose—now known in the nursery as "Rikki-tikki-tavi"—is a fairly decent citizen, and it fits into the time-worn economy of that region without a jar. Its specialty is killing cobras and devouring them. In an evil moment, the mongoose was introduced in the islands of Barbadoes and Jamaica, to clear out the rats that were troubling the cane-fields. In quick time the rats were exterminated, and then the mongooses ambitiously looked about for more food and more worlds to conquer. With cheerful impartiality they devoured the snakes and lizards, wild birds and poultry, cleaned out every living thing that they could catch and kill, and then began on the sugar-cane. The last count in this indictment seems hard to believe, but it is a fact that when hard-pressed by hunger the mongoose freely devours fruit and vegetable food.

Up to this date, the mongoose has invaded and become a destructive pest in Barbadoes, Jamaica, Cuba, St. Vincent, St. Lucia, Trinidad, Nevis, Fiji and all the larger islands of the Hawaiian group. Everywhere its progress is the same—devouring rats, snakes, wild birds, small mammals, poultry, fruit and vegetables.

The fierce temper, matchless courage and all-embracing appetite of the mongoose would render its transplantation into any of the warmer portions of America a terrible calamity. In the southern states, from the Carolinas to California, and up the Pacific coast as far as Seattle, it could live, thrive and multiply; and the slaughter that it would inflict upon our wild life, especially quail, grouse and wild turkeys, would drive the American people crazy.

The importation of the mongoose into the United States is forbidden by a federal law; but for all that, Lascars from eastern ships frequently smuggle them in, in their bags of clothing or inside their shirts.   Fancy an animal with the murderous ferocity of a mink, the agility of a squirrel, the penetration of a ferret and the cunning of a rat, infesting our thickets and barnyards.   The mongoose can live in the South wherever a rat, raccoon or opossum can live; and not for a million dollars could any one of the southern or Pacific states afford to have a pair of those little gray fiends imported and set free.   If such a calamity ever should occur, all wheels should stop until the calamity-breeders were caught and pulverized.   If *Herpestes griseus* ever finds a real lodgment in any state or national forest, or in any private forest, the forest rangers will then be called upon to fight the worst pest that ever fastened upon our country.

In concluding this subject, we wish to point out the fact that on the subject of pests and *alleged* pests among wild birds and mammals, there are endless opportunities for differences of opinion. The handling of the questions that will arise before every forester calls for calm judgment and a judicial mind that is open to conviction, but is not to be swayed by every wave of local resentment or emotion.   In every case of doubt, the young judge must bear in mind the wise injunction of Holy Writ, which says: "Prove all things; hold fast that which is good."

CHAPTER V

THE DUTY AND POWER OF THE CITIZEN IN WILD LIFE PROTECTION

We now have reached a subject which is the conclusion of the whole matter of wild-life destruction and conservation,—the duty of the citizen. Upon the response, or the lack of response, to the call that now is being made to the intelligent conscience of America and Europe hangs the fate of the best and most valuable wild life of the world. If that wild life is not saved through the initiative and the sacrifices of private individuals, it will not be saved.

Let us make a cold-blooded analysis of the situation.

We know that throughout all portions of the globe that are really occupied by civilized man, or his agents, the slaughter of wild life is proceeding in wholesale ways and at a fearful pace.

We know that already a very great many species of highly valuable birds and mammals have been locally exterminated over immense areas.

We know that during our own times, a number of species have been totally exterminated, actually under our eyes. The total list is so long that I have not even attempted to give it.

We know that the deadliness of firearms and the number of firearms are constantly being increased.

We know that the thirst for the blood of wild creatures now amounts to an insatiable rage; a "craze" in fact, as well as in name. There are a thousand rich men in America, young and old, each of whom would willingly go to the gates of hades itself in order to find his chosen game.

Finally, we know that of the millions of men who form the army of destruction, not more than 5 per cent of them care one iota about our duty to posterity or the claims of our children and grandchildren. In the saving of game for posterity, by their own volition and unrestrained by law, the great majority of men and boys who shoot, including all in America and in Europe, have no more mercy or sense of honor toward wild life than so many gray wolves of the prairies.

In the United States there are about 5,000,000 gunners, game-hogs and sportsmen. In that entire multitude I venture to say that there are not over 2,000 men or boys who by reason of *their own high principles* could be trusted in any country to hunt wild game *wholly unrestrained by the hand of the law*. I mention this fact, not merely as a complaint against the men I accuse, but because it *is* a fact, and it now is a factor of tremendous importance to all those who desire to preserve wild life as a duty to posterity. In order to plan our campaign of offense against the army of destruction, it is a mili-

All succeeding generations; future mankind

tary necessity that we should know the composition and numerical strength of the enemy.

As a sort of voucher for the character of my statements regarding the army of destruction, I desire to state that during the past twenty years I have come in personal touch with thousands of men who shoot and thousands of real wild-life protectors. My personal acquaintance with the men who kill wild creatures covers the best hunting-grounds of two hemispheres, and from this acquaintance I have learned the true sentiments toward wild life of several thousand men. As this acquaintance has progressed, I have met one surprise and shock after another. My original, optimistic and too liberal opinion of the sentiments of the men who shoot game has steadily and rapidly gone down. To-day, I know that there are in the ranks of the men who shoot game a very few men,—let us be very liberal and say 5 per cent,—who are noble-hearted, high-minded, awake to their duty toward wild life and to posterity, and willing to make real sacrifices in order to do their duty.

But the 95 per cent are utterly contemptuous of their duty whenever the saving of wild life involves a *real, personal sacrifice.* Twenty per cent of them virtuously stop shooting and hang up their guns— when the game is so reduced that there is no longer a good bag to be had! The remaining 75 per cent will go right on shooting, down to the very last bird of a species, *so long as the law permits it!*

Now, that is a grim and ugly picture. I wish it were untrue; but it is not. Seventy-five per cent of the men who shoot game in America, in Europe, Asia and Africa are thoroughly sordid, selfish and merciless, both toward the game and toward posterity. As a rule, nothing can induce any of them to make any voluntary sacrifices for the preservation cause. They stop for nothing save the law.

The time was when I was proud of being known as a sportsman; but that time has gone by, forever. The conscientious and duty-doing sportsmen of the world are now so hopelessly mixed up with the motley array of game-hogs and gunners-at-large as to be almost unrecognizable. There are in the United States about six clubs of sportsmen to which it is an honor to belong, but that is all.

This ugly sore spot is laid bare in order that the real friends of wild life may know the worst, and may at the outset realize the painful fact that the men who hunt and kill wild game are not preserving wild game to-day for any other reason than that they may kill it to-morrow. The army of destruction will *not* preserve our birds and mammals as a duty to posterity. The people who do not shoot have far too long left the protection of our birds and quadrupeds to the men who do shoot! As a result, look at Ohio, Illinois, Indiana, Iowa, Minnesota and Kansas,—almost gameless!

We must make an end to the folly of abandoning 154 species of our finest birds to the merciless treat-

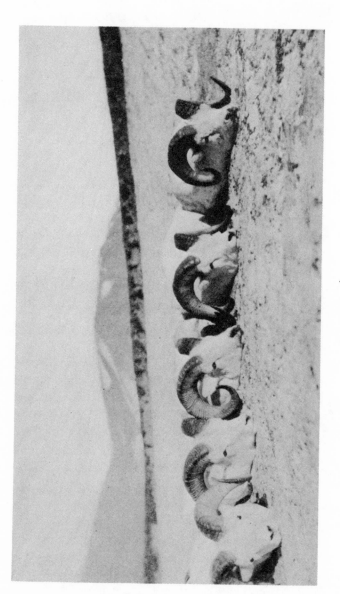

ALASKA, ANY YEAR

Why the White Mountain Sheep are fast disappearing!

ment of the men who kill game-birds. Do sensible
shepherds set wolves to guard their flocks? Take a
lantern, like Diogenes, go out, and see if you can
find a sportsman who *voluntarily* makes any sacrifice for the good of the birds, or who does more than
preserve to-day in order to kill to-morrow. See if
you can find in your city more than five men who
shoot who will subscribe $50 each in order to pro-
mote a movement to give the quail remnant of the
state a five-year close season. Show me the cities
of the United States in which a campaigner will
not wear out a dollar's worth of shoe-leather for
every dollar that he raises by subscription *among
gunners* for real wild-life protection. I think the
total number can be counted on the fingers and
thumb of one hand.

The point of this story is that if the remnants of
the wild life of North America are saved to posterity, they must be saved by the efforts and the
sacrifices of men and women who do not kill wild
creatures.

We hold that the real men and women of to-day
owe to posterity a duty in the preservation of wild
life than can not conscientiously be ignored. The
wild life of the world is not ours, to dispose of
wholly as we please. We hold it *in trust,* for the
benefit of ourselves, and equal benefits to those who
come after us. As honorable guardians we have no
right to waste and squander the heritage of our

children and grandchildren. It is our duty to stay the hand that strives to apply the torch.

We received from the hand of Nature a marvelous continent, overflowing with an abundance of wild life. But we do not own it all; and it is not all ours to destroy if we choose. Nature was a million years, or more, in developing the picturesque moose, the odd mountain goat and the unique antelope. Shall we destroy and exterminate those species in one brief century? The young Americans of the year 2014 will read of those wonderful creatures, and if they find none of them alive how will they characterize the men of 1914? I, for one, do not wish in 2014 to be classed with the swine of Mauritius that exterminated the dodo.

The most advanced educators of America are awake to the vital necessity of forest conservation. The twenty-one forestry schools now in existence in our country have for their foundations the necessity for forest conservation. Educators and statesmen, and the men of means who support good works, all are awake to the vital necessity of systematic effort in arresting the march of forest destruction and providing for the perpetuation of our forest wealth. If by neglect of duty we were to allow the vandals to sweep off all timber from the United States during the present century, we would be regarded as monsters. Fifty years hence, our children would blush for their parents. And yet, in effect, through our mistaken principles and the dominant influence of the destroyers, we are now, at this hour, permitting and witnessing the annihilation of our game-birds and game-quadrupeds, everywhere in the United States outside of a very few *real* preserves. If my iteration of this fact is likely to be regarded as tiresome, it should be remembered that only the quick awakening of this nation, and the quick application of stern remedies, can save the patient.

Perhaps there are those who believe that the various state game commissions are to be held responsible for the saving of our wild life. It may be said that they have power, they have state funds at their command, they are supposed to have the means of enforcing the laws. In view of the state game commissions, why (it may be asked) should the duty of saving the wild life devolve upon the private citizen? Let us answer categorically.

First. The real business of every state game commission is to enforce the laws that it finds upon the statute books. All other activities are quite secondary.

Second. Every wise state game commission is animated by a desire to do for the wild life of the state the very best that it can do under the circumstances, and at the same time assist in securing betterments in laws and in law enforcement.

Third. No state game commission dares go to extremes in demanding more drastic protective laws, because to do so means incurring the open,

*active hostility of thousands of gunners who are
ever ready to fight for their killing privileges, even
unto the destruction of their own game commission.
Any game commissioner who defies that body of
men, in order to do his duty, takes his official life in
his hands and must expect to meet his enemies in a
death grapple before his legislature.*

*Fourth. It is only the strongest of the state
game commissions, those whose members are
assured of strong outside support, who dare to
advocate before their legislatures the drastic measure which alone will serve to save the present wild-
life situation.*

Private citizens and humanitarian organizations
must not think that all the work and all the fighting
for the saving of wild life should be done, or can be
done, by the state game commissions. That demand
would be unfair and its *adequate* fulfilment quite
impossible. The drastic and unpopular measures,
such as stopping the sale of game, the conferring of
long close seasons and the stoppage of all hunting
in the national forests, should originate with outside
men, who are not open to vengeful assaults by
gunners, and who can say what they please in support of their cause. These independent promoters
of wild-life protection measures *always* receive the
hearty support of their respective state game commissions, but the arrangement saves the latter from
being converted into targets for universal assault.

I do not mean to imply that state game commissions *never* take the initiative in securing strong measures. Far from it. Very many of the best measures now on the statute books were placed there through their initiative. Among the fighting game commissions of my close acquaintance I mention particularly, with pride and satisfaction, that of Pennsylvania, headed by Dr. Kalbfus and Commissioner John M. Phillips; the New Jersey Commission, headed by Mr. Ernest Napier; the Massachusetts Commission, headed by Dr. George W. Field, and the California Commission, led by Mr. Ernest Schaeffle, secretary. At this very hour, the California Commission and its thousands of supporters are engaged in a bitter struggle against the largest and most shameless body of wild-life destroyers to be found in any one state. The destroyers, to the number of 30,000 or more, are determined to drain the blood of the wild birds of California down to the very last drop, regardless of the rights of future Californians, regardless of precedents set by other states and in defiance of the wishes of the vast majority of the people of the state. A band of alien-born game-dealers is attempting to ride roughshod over the decent people of California, and at the same time destroy one of the best state game-laws in the United States.

Without the active and constant support of private citizens, the California Game and Fish Commission would long ago have been utterly vanquished; but with that support, it will continue.

In the protection of wild life, it seems to me that the average citizen does not even begin to realize his own power. I know it, and a great many other men know it, because we have seen the results that have been accomplished by the private citizen on the firing-line. If the defenders of wild life can succeed in reaching and arousing the private citizen, the wild life of our country can even yet be saved from the general annihilation that threatens it. The appeal for new help must be made to the men and women of America who do not go hunting, and *who do not kill wild creatures!*

Speaking generally, I think that we have gone with the gunners about as far as we can go. I fear that they will concede *no more* than they already have conceded, and the new measures they are willing to concede I believe are utterly inadequate to the saving of our wild life. As a class and a mass, the gunners are unwilling to grant long close seasons, of five or ten years, and therefore we must secure those long close seasons without their aid!

We have proven what can be done by turning to humanitarians at large—the big-hearted people who spend much of their lives in building hospitals, endowing schools and caring for poor humanity in general. These are the men and women who care about posterity and its rights, as well as about the needy ones of to-day. It was the 50,000 women of the United States, organized and unorganized, who rushed the anti-feather-millinery clause through the

United States Senate in spite of an opposing majority in the dominant party. It was the zoölogists of the University of California who in 1912 started the fight to save the birds of California, and in 1913 won a substantial victory.

It was the men of the Camp-Fire Club of America who in 1910, as private citizens, went before the United States Senate, demanding the adoption of three rational, common-sense measures for the preservation of our once valuable fur-seal industry from total annihilation. It was the final adoption of those three measures that *did* save to this nation a national commercial asset, worth millions of dollars. But for the action of that Camp-Fire Club of private citizens it is absolutely certain that by this time the fur-seal remnant would have been practically annihilated.

Assuming that the duty of the private citizen toward wild life is conceded, how can that duty best be discharged, and how can every unit of interest be made effective?

In the first place, the citizen must make up his mind that a real performance of his duty will involve some sacrifices on his part, either in effort or in money, or both. There is no royal road to the perfect protection of wild life. Results that are of far-reaching importance, and that are worth while, always involve hard thinking, hard labor and the expenditure of money.

The first duty of the wild-life protectionist is to inform himself adequately regarding the leading issues of the day in the protection field. Knowledge is power, and a protagonist of wild life badly informed is like a knightly champion wearing only half a suit of armor. Good sources of information are your state game commission, the United States Biological Survey of the Department of Agriculture, the magazines for sportsmen, two books by Mr. E. H. Forbush of Boston, and another book entitled "Our Vanishing Wild Life." Any man or woman, anywhere in the United States, who is willing to lend a hand but is at loss to know what to do, need only declare that willingness in order to be advised what cause to espouse.

The accomplishment of a great reform nearly always means the enactment of new laws in the face of strong opposition. Every *great* reform always treads on a great many toes; and the owners of many of those toes will not only cry out, but many of them will fight. A bill to stop the sale of game always arouses the opposition of the market-gunners, the game-dealers and the hotel and restaurant interests. The game-dealers are natural fighters, and in fighting for their selling privileges they hire lawyers in abundance and spend money liberally. As business men, they know how to appeal to the business men in any legislature, and their opposition is a very serious matter. The way to counteract it is to *overwhelm it,* in the legislature

and before the governor, with appeals and demands
from the press and from men and women who have
no selfish interests to serve and no axes to grind, in
behalf of imperiled nature. Men who are moved
to leave their mirth and their employment, and
journey to their state capitol to appear at hearings
before committees in behalf of the wild life of the
people at large, always command very respectful
attention, and in about nineteen cases out of every
twenty, if the cause of the people is *adequately
represented,* the friends of wild life do not appeal in
vain.

At this point I wish to offer an observation in
regard to legislative campaign work. There is
lobbying and lobbying—two distinct kinds. The
common variety is that which has an ax to grind, a
personal interest to promote or protect, a commercial end to serve. With this brand, many legislators have little patience, and the ax-grinding
lobbyist often finds his way blocked by stern laws
and rules.

But the lobbyist who goes up for the good of the
people is in a very different class. His lobbying is
not only respectable, but honorable; and to him all
doors are open. He is treated well; always with
respect, frequently with deference. He has a
powerful advantage over the man who for the sake
of making more money is begging that bird-
slaughter be continued. I think that our clause for
the exclusion of feather millinery was inserted in

the tariff bill partly because of the fact that its
advocates were the only persons who appeared
before the Ways and Means Committee of the
House who were *not* seeking to serve personal and
selfish ends! The novelty of that appearance was
so great that our appeal had to be granted!

I have known a few state game commissioners
and others who, in their early experiences, have
hesitated to enter legislative lobbies in behalf of
their measures. To all persons who feel inclined to
shrink from this line of duty toward wild life we
may paraphrase an ancient and excellent precept,
thus: There is no excellence without great lobbying.
I have taken many chances in various legislative
halls, and most of all in Congress. I have felt it
my duty to appear before legislative committees of
a number of states, and never once have I been
accused of intrusion, or violation of state rights, or
of advocating a bad cause.

> " Thrice is he arm'd that hath his quarrel just;
>   And he but naked, though lock'd up in steel,
>   Whose conscience with injustice is corrupted."

Every forester in the United States should feel
that lobbying for conservation causes is the very
highest line of duty in which it is possible for him
to engage. No man can so well advocate the repeal
of a bad forest or game law, or the enactment of a
good law, as the man who comes in personal contact
with its working effect. Legislators like to have

come before them practical men, who know all the facts, and who know whereof they speak. I have in mind a celebrated case wherein an international fishery commission sent to Congress a wrong conclusion. Three hard-handed fishermen of Put-in-Bay journeyed down to Washington, taking with them a pail of water, three live fish and a section of fish-net. With that simple outfit in a five-minute demonstration before a Congressional committee they upset forever the unwise conclusions of an international commission, and the whole subject was reopened on a new basis.

It is impossible for me to state with sufficient emphasis the necessity for *immediate action* and *quick results* in the saving of wild life. The assaults that are being made on the forests of the United States are in no way comparable with it. At one swoop the creation of vast national forest reserves arrests the hands of the timber destroyer; but there are no such corresponding reserved areas for wild life. Beside the vast extent of the reserved forests, the national parks and game-preserves are lost in utter insignificance.

Already a great amount of basic educational work for wild life has been done. There are few intelligent persons to whom the subject is new. The public mind now is so sensitive to impressions regarding wild life it is possible to secure, by a few months of effort, results that even five years ago were wildly impossible. Our task to-day is not the educating of the masses, but the arousing of the conscientious citizen to the point of positive action.

In these days we know not who will be the next man to develop into a leader of conservation campaigns. This being the case, it becomes of interest to know what the young conservationist can do when the mantle of leadership has fallen upon him.

The greatest coups are to be made in securing the enactment of new laws that produce sweeping reforms. To the young leader I would say, *never choose a trivial cause,* but instead, choose each time one that is worth while to grown men. It takes but little more time to pass a large bill than is necessary for a small one; and big men always prefer to be identified with big measures. Do not rush to the legislature with a demand for a law to permit the taking of bullheads with June-bugs in the creeks of your township, or to give your county a specially early open season on quail in order that your brother may try his new gun before he goes back to college. *Do not propose any local legislation;* for bills of that species are coming strongly into disfavor with lawmakers.

One determined man who is reasonably intelligent can promote and direct a movement that will secure the enactment of a new law, provided he is industrious and sufficiently determined. The man who starts a movement must make up his mind to follow it up, direct its fortunes, stay with it when the storms of criticism and opposition beat upon it, and never give up until it is signed by the Governor or the President. A leader must be willing to sacrifice his personal convenience, the most of his pleasures, and keep at his work when his friends are asleep or at the theater.

The first step in starting a new campaign is to raise the fund with which to meet its expenses. Expense money is absolutely necessary, or the amount of printing, posting, telegraphing and traveling will be extremely limited. Good men who give their time and gray matter must not be expected or permitted to pay their expenses from their own pockets. A little later we will have more to say on this point.

A short bill can be drawn by your own member of the lawmaking body; but a long one, that requires study and research, must be drawn by a good lawyer, who must be paid something for his time. Every bill should recognize existing laws, either to repeal or to amend, and it must be either prohibitory or permissive. This means that the new law desired must say what shall not be done, or else what may be done lawfully, all other acts being forbidden. I prefer the prohibitive form, as being the more impressive, and also most easily provided with penalties.

As soon as a bill is introduced in a legislative body it is referred to a committee, for consideration and report; and a favorable committee report is highly essential to success.

It is at this point that the citizen at large looms upon the scene and begins to play his part. The leader will ask the committee for a public hearing, which will be granted, for a date fixed well in advance. Then the leader sends out his printed matter, broadcast, and calls upon the people at large for support. On the date fixed for the hearing, a large delegation appears, representing all sorts and conditions of men. A list of speakers has been carefully prepared and handed to the sponsor of the measure. The opposition should be heard first, and in nine cases out of ten, the opposition will contain chiefly men who have private interests to serve, and their attorneys.

From this point onward, the friends of the measure, all over the state or the nation, should write to their representatives in the legislature or in Congress, stating their views of the bill,— always in their own language and never in machine-made letters,—asking that it be supported. The press must be vigorously invited and urged to help the cause, and all necessary facts must be furnished in order that the editorial mind may be able to judge the case on its own merits.

The larger the measure, the greater is the certainty that it will affect adversely some large commercial interests, or that it will interfere with the special privileges of a large class of selfish persons. Every large measure is certain to be opposed by numerous enemies. When the time arrives to advo-

cate before Congress *the conversion of every
national forest into a national game-preserve,* there
will be a great outcry from the resident hunters
who for years have been exploiting those forests as
their private hunting-grounds.   Then must the
People-at-Large, the great, silent, sleepy, but irresistible mass, arouse, shake off their lethargy, and
unite in demanding their rights, in behalf of themselves, and posterity.   The enemies of conservation,
who wish to see Nature stripped bare of her
resources for the benefit of their "constituents," will
declaim and protest, just as they did against the
enactment of the federal migratory bird law.   But
they will be overwhelmed, just as its fifteen opponents in the House of Representatives were overwhelmed in May, 1913, when they attempted to
block the wheels of the car of Progress on which
the McLean bill was rolling through the United
States Congress.   That must be our next great
victory, and in the winning of it, thousands of
strong college men will be needed on the firing-line.
Will the men of Yale take the initiative in enlisting
that contingent, and in helping to raise the flag of
conservation higher than ever before—so high, in
fact, that it will make the destructionists dizzy to
look at it?

Let the citizen remember that several great wild-
life protection causes have been finally won through
Congress, and through state legislatures, by the
personal letters of constituents addressed in earnest

appeal to their representatives and senators. Any
cause that can command the support of 20,000 or
30,000, or 100,000 strong personal letters from
constituents is backed by a force that is well-nigh
irresistible. Sometimes "the voice of the people"
is indeed "the voice of God." In the passage of the
Lacey bird law, the Bayne law, the McLean-Weeks
law and the plumage law, the opposition of private
and commercial interests was in the end completely
overwhelmed by the tens of thousands of earnest
letters of appeal and demand that flowed in an
irresistible tide upon the lawmakers. I wish that
the college men of America would make clear to all
persons in their spheres of influence the power of
the *original* personal letter from constituent to
representative. At the same time, it should be
remembered that "machine-made" letters always
are detectable; they are worse than useless, and it
is right that they should be so.

There is another phase of citizen duty toward
wild life that I approach with a feeling of hopeless
despair. It is the raising of campaign funds. I
present it merely as a matter of form, and not at all
in the hope of accomplishing even secondary results.

In all campaigns for the protection and increase
of wild life, the need for campaign cash is very
great. I have seen three great causes won because
each one had an adequate campaign fund. I have
seen several worthy movements languish and die of
financial starvation. At this moment I know of

three causes of moment that are almost destitute of funds. Last winter the war-chest of the defenders of wild life in Virginia, where a gallant fight was being made, was down to $18, until it was replenished by the New York Zoölogical Society.

The trouble is that very, *very* few men and women, even among the fabulously rich, are willing to give anything substantial to the wild-life cause. As a result, our cause is financially on a half-starvation basis, and seems likely to remain so. On this whole continent, only two persons ever have given sums for the wild-life cause that require six figures to express them. Mr. Albert Wilcox gave, in his will, $322,000 to the National Association of Audubon Societies, as an endowment fund for its work; and Mrs. Russell Sage paid $150,000 for Marsh Island, Louisiana, as a permanent bird sanctuary for the winter use of northern migratory birds. To other wild-life protection causes Mrs. Sage has given at least $50,000 more. From these sums, the cash gifts for wild life fall at one deep plunge down to $10,000, and not more than ten persons ever have given so much as that sum. Perhaps twenty persons have given $5,000 each, about forty have given $1,000 each and from that the figures rapidly dwindle down to $5, $2 and $1.

Everyone knows that in war the men in the trenches and on the firing-line are not supposed to provide the sinews of war that come from the paymaster's chest. In civilized wars, the noncom-

batants provide the war funds. In our warfare for
the saving of wild life, the men on the firing-line
who battle for great new measures usually are compelled to finance themselves. Much of the time
that they should spend in harassing the enemy is
spent in begging, hat in hand, for the few dollars
that are necessary to pay campaign expenses from
day to day.

The trouble is that, as a rule, the men who kill
wild life sullenly refuse to make *any* real sacrifices
in cash for the benefit of the faunas they have helped
to destroy; and the people who do not kill wild
creatures are interested in other causes. The
latter feel that they are not to blame for any of the
destruction, and they do not understand why they
should be expected to make sacrifices for wild life.

Unfortunately, the need of money for campaign
expenses in behalf of wild life never before has been
one-half as great as it is now. The destroyers of
wild life are wide awake to the dangers that
threaten their killing privileges, and they have
acquired the habit of furnishing money and hiring
attorneys to oppose the cause of protection.

The friends of wild life need money in every
campaign. They need it to pay the cost of printing,
postage, telegraphing, traveling expenses, and services that can not be procured for nothing. With
sufficient campaign funds and reasonably able
generalship, *any* wild-life cause can be won! I urge
the friends of wild life to acquire the habit of giving

money for campaign purposes, in liberal figures,
and of asking others to give. To beg for a good
cause of any kind is not only right but honorable;
for it is ten times more painful to ask for many
subscriptions than it is to make one subscription and
thereby purchase immunity. Any man can fight
for wild life, but it takes a real hero to raise money
for it by subscription.

The saving of the wild life and forests of the
world is a *duty* that by no means is confined to a
small group of persons who work for nothing and
subsist on their own enthusiasm. The saving of
the fauna of a nation is a national task. It is literally everybody's business. It rests upon the shoul-
ders of the educated and the intelligent, and the
motives that prompt it are not found in the breasts
of the sordid and the ignorant. The educated
people of the United States and Canada now are
called upon to protect *their own* from the Goths
and Vandals of the army of destruction who are
strangers to the higher sentiments.

In some of the states of our country, it is worse
than futile to rely for the saving of wild life upon
the men who kill. They are devoted to slaughter,
and it is a waste of time to talk with them. Turn
we, therefore, to the great body of humane men and
women who do *not* go hunting and *who do not kill*.

We have a right to demand services for this
great cause from the educators, the scientists, the
zoölogists in particular; from lawyers and doctors

and merchants; and above all, from editors. Intelligent people who ignore this cause fall short of their duty to humanity and to themselves. The universities and colleges, the high schools and the normal schools, all have it in their power to exert an enormous influence in this cause. Think what it would mean if 30 per cent of the annual graduates of all American institutions of learning should go forth well informed on the details of this work, and fully resolved to spread the doctrine of conservation, far and near! And think, also, what it would mean if even one-half the men and women who earn their daily bread in the field of zoölogy and nature-study should elect to make this cause their own! And yet, I tell you that in spite of an appeal for help, dating as far back as 1898, fully 90 per cent of the zoölogists of America stick closely to their desk-work, soaring after the infinite and diving after the unfathomable, but never spending a dollar or lifting an active finger on the firing-line in defense of wild life. I have talked to these men until I am tired; and the most of them seem to be hopelessly sodden and apathetic.

While this is equally true of educators at large, the fact is they are *far* less to blame for present conditions than are many American zoölogists. The latter have upon them obligations such as no man can escape without being shamefully derelict. Fancy an ornithologist studying feather arrangement, or avian osteology, or the distribution of subspecies, while the guns of the game-hogs are roaring all around him and strings of bobolinks are coming into the markets for sale! Yet that is precisely what is happening in many portions of America to-day; and I tell you that if the birds of North America are saved, it will not be by the ornithologists at large. But fortunately there are a few noble exceptions to this ghastly general rule.

The people of America who have money to give away to causes for the betterment of humanity should consider the campaigns that are being made, and that should be made, to save the remainder of our wild life for the benefit of mankind at large. This cause is entitled to a share of betterment funds, and it should *not* be compelled to live on the husks and crumbs that fall from the million-dollar tables of other causes. The sight of scores of causes and institutions struggling with undigested wealth, while the wild life of the world is being swept away, and its defenders are working on a starvation basis, is fairly maddening.

With a fair amount of campaign money, the wild life of the world could be saved: but the giving of money to that cause is not fashionable. Is it because the individual glory to be derived from it is too small? There are in all the world only three endowment funds for the benefit of wild life. One contains $340,000, another, $51,205 and the third, $5,000. Perhaps by the time the wild birds and

beasts are all gone, and it is entirely too late, some
one will devote a really large sum to salvage work.

Before leaving this branch of our subject, I
desire to reveal one fact that may be useful.
The college-graduate-with-a-keen-conscience never
knows when a public need will leap upon his shoul-
ders and settle there, to be dislodged only through
personal effort in the line of imperative duty. He
never knows when he will be seized and impressed
into service by a cause. The chances are that
the men of the forest schools will be driven by
conservation causes.

It is a popular idea that to solicit funds by subscription is a painful task. Carried out beyond
two digits, it does become so. Under ordinary circumstances, there is no calling more honorable than
soliciting funds for good causes. The solicitor has
no occasion to apologize because he is asking. It is
the solicited who apologizes when he is unable to
respond. During the past five years I have raised
much wild-life money by subscription, and I have
received scores of letters (with checks enclosed)
thanking me for having given the writers an opportunity to join in good work for wild life! Write a
strong circular, state the case clearly and ask with
brisk confidence that the person addressed will bear
his share of the general burden. In a thoroughly
good cause, a strongly worded printed circular,
sent under seal, is a good method. For separating
the sheep from the goats, there is nothing equal to

the raising of funds for wild-life protection. It is a blood test to which only the red-blooded and the high-minded ever respond.

The greatest of all obstacles in the way of the conservator of wild life and forests is the deadly American spirit of restless and heedless wastefulness. The American continent has been developed by men who, time after time, settled down, robbed the soil of its fertility, then moved on westward to new lands. The American national spirit is for quick, wasteful *conquest,* not calm and patient conservation. It is our way to cut down, slash up, kill, lay waste, get rich quick,—and a fig for posterity! Our rich men strive to leave great fortunes in cash to their children, but they rarely reforest or restore wild life. That is too slow for them.

The forest champions of America now are making a Herculean effort to instill into the American mind the idea of the systematic replanting of denuded forest lands: but it is like rolling a huge stone up a steep hill. Quite recently I journeyed through several hundred miles of southern pine forests, always watching for signs of systematic reforestation, but not once did I see a pine, young or old, that clearly appeared to have been planted by the hand of man. In the denuded forest areas of Florida, Georgia, the Carolinas and Virginia, nature was bravely struggling to restore what man had greedily destroyed, but not once did I see a single acre on which nature was being assisted by man.

None are so blind as those who will not see. It is impossible to place ideas mechanically within empty minds. Sometimes the inertia of ignorance is as fixed and immovable as the foundations of Mount Washington. At other times, it slowly yields to persistent education. Just how many generations are necessary to transform a confirmed tree-cutter into a true forest conservator remains to be seen.

The preservation and increase of the forests is a very different matter from the salvage of the birds and beasts. Man and nature, jointly or severally, can replant a denuded forest, and the lapse of time will bring the renaissance. With forests, there is a modicum of time available in which to act. With wild life, it is a case of now or never. *A fauna once destroyed can not be brought back!* The destroyers of wild life are so omnipresent, persistent and relentless that the defenders and preservers must act at once, or very soon it will be hopelessly too late. No power on earth can repopulate China with the wild species that were hers when she had forests, and before the era of extermination.

Of the many blighting influences that bear down upon wild life, and promote its destruction, one of the most serious is local disregard for protective laws, and the disloyalty of juries, and sometimes of judges, also, to their sworn duty. In the western

RESULT OF A FEW HOURS' TROUT FISHING NEAR SPOKANE, WASH.

Another line of extermination according to law. Three times too many fish for one rod. In those cold mountain streams, fish grow slowly, and a stream is quickly "Fished out."

third of the United States, and especially on the
so-called "frontier," it is a common occurrence for
a sympathetic jury of neighbors and friends to
acquit a red-handed violator of the game-law by
saying: "Not guilty! He needed the meat."

Sometimes a judge on the bench calmly elects to
turn loose without punishment a man who should
pay the full penalty for his misdeeds and his contempt of the law. The latest and most disappoint-
ing case occurred in Key West, Florida. Three
men were caught in the act of raiding the protected
egret rookery at Alligator Bay, on the west coast of
Florida. By the expenditure of great efforts and
much public funds, the offenders were finally taken
to Key West, a distance of about one hundred
miles. It is stated that the judge before whom they
should have been tried kindly *advised* that the
accused men be set free. Recognizing the utter
futility of bringing the men to trial, the game
wardens and the prosecuting attorney had no
recourse but to abandon the case. The men were
set free; and now it is reported that they have
announced their intention to "clean out" that
rookery in the coming nesting season.

Any community which tolerates contempt for law,
and law-defying judges, is in a degenerate state,
bordering on barbarism; and in the United States
there are literally *thousands* of such communities!
The thoroughness with which one lawless individual
who goes unwhipped by justice can create contempt

for law and demoralize a whole neighborhood is both remarkable and deplorable. That way lies anarchy. In such a community, any upright man who boldly denounces lawlessness and upholds the majesty of the law is not only the best citizen of that community, but he is also a public benefactor.

About 60 per cent of the American people are like sheep—always ready to follow the boldest leader and be swayed by the strongest man. This being true, the duty of the good citizen to openly and insistently demand the observance of the law is, in every lawless community, quite as imperative as his duty to cast his ballot on election day.

One determined man who is right can face without fear one hundred who are wrong. Such a man has the right to demand the support of all good citizens. Were I a game warden, or a forester with a game warden's authority, I would, as my first act, print and post a proclamation calling upon all men of lawless tendencies to obey the law, and also calling upon all good citizens to give me their active support in securing obedience to the law.

In Putnam County, New York, in 1913 we saw a county-wide vote-selling industry of many years standing and great popularity absolutely stamped out through the moral courage, determination and aggressive industry of one private individual, Mr. Thomas M. Upp, who accomplished his task almost unaided, save by the local newspapers.

A lawless community, whether in New York or

in Alaska, is to all good citizens a source of irritation, a public nuisance and a danger that requires
abatement. That abatement should be peaceable
if possible, but forcible if necessary. If education
and appeal can not work the necessary reform, then
the stern execution of the law is the next recourse.
It is high time that sneering at game laws and game
wardens should be regarded as intolerable, and
sternly suppressed; for contempt for law usually
breeds serious trouble for some one.

When left wholly to himself, savage man does
not inflict useless wholesale slaughter upon the wild
beasts and birds; but in the ranks of civilized men
there are degenerates who love slaughter and promote it with joy and exultation. If it happens to be
quite useless, no matter! At all events, it makes a
thrilling story.

Henceforth, our hope for arresting the efforts of
the slaughterers must rest upon the hitherto silent
majority of men, and women also, who abhor
slaughter, and do not kill. They outnumber the
army of destruction at least 9 to 1. Their potential influence is beyond the reach of calculation.
They can do for wild life well nigh whatever they
choose. The time has come when they must be
called upon to take up their share of the white
man's burden, and bear it to the goal. No man who
cares a pin's price for the heritage of his children
can remain indifferent to the cause of wild-life
preservation or forest conservation. Each man of

conscience may be permitted to take his choice of three kinds of tasks, three species of burdens. They are *labor, publicity* or *money;* and he who chooses one of these, and bears it like a man, may claim immunity from the other two.

It occurs to me to insert here a word of advice to every forester and teacher of foresters. Many a sportsman will say: "I have no occasion to aid your cause. I contribute annually, in the form of a fee for my hunting license."

Now that plea is absolutely hollow. The sportsman who pays annually the magnificent sum of $1, or even $50, for a local license to hunt is merely contributing to the pay of wardens to protect his game from the other gunner until he himself can reach it, and kill it! That is all. That endless chain of saving to-day and killing to-morrow does not *increase* the wild life of a state; not in the least. On the contrary, that is the great American process of extermination according to law!

To the men of Yale, I repeat at the end what I said at the beginning: *Noblesse oblige!* The nobility conferred by a university or college or high-school education brings with it solemn obligations which no high-minded citizen can ignore. Some of these obligations trend toward distressed wild life. Only personal effort can discharge them to the satisfaction of a properly sensitized conscience. Do not think to discharge any of your obligations to man or to nature by telling some one else what to do.

Every year, about a thousand men who have been jarred, virtuously seek to salve their consciences by writing to me, and pointing out what *I* should do next! Such men are a weariness to the flesh. In sixty seconds a child in wild-life protection can block out tasks that would keep an army of men busy for an entire year. We can do such a thing now, in about twenty-five words, thus:

Have Congress enact a law making every national forest a hard-and-fast game preserve, with all hunting forever prohibited, save of predatory animals.

As every human heart knoweth its own bitterness, so does every state of the American nation know its own sins of omission and commission respecting the wild life within its borders. I know that they know, because the black list has been printed in a book, and sent to each member of each legislature. Much as has been done in wild-life conservation during the past five years, the amount that remains to be done is appalling; and the shameless repealer of good laws, like the poor of Holy Writ, we have with us always.

It is high time for the great universities and colleges of our country seriously to enter upon the work—aye, let me say the *drudgery,* for that it is— of wild-life conservation. The majority of our zoölogists are engrossed in charming zoölogical studies while the everyday birds and beasts of their country are being swept away. As a class and a mass, they are a doubtful asset. The few exceptions only prove the rule.

Turn we, therefore, to the open-eyed, open-minded general educators and general students, and lay before them the appeal of the wild. Shall all our best wild life be swept away, until nothing remains save noxious insects, rats and mice? Shall our forests, our orchards, gardens and grain-fields be presented bodily to the insect world? Shall the dignified chase of deer and bear, the wild turkey and ruffed grouse, degenerate, as it has in Italy, to the popping of robins, sparrows and bobolinks? Already our sweethearts and wives are wearing skunk-skin and rabbit-skin furs, where once they wore sable, otter and beaver. We are presenting annually to the insect world about $500,000,000 worth of our valuable products. Does this appeal to the thoughtful mind, or not?

The facts and figures that I have endeavored to place before you are no figments of a fevered imagination. They are incontestably true. The conclusions to be drawn from them are inexorable. The saving of our wild life is not an academic cause, or an optional study. It is a burning question of the market-basket and the dinner-pail. The great question to-day is: Will the American people now rise to the occasion, and prosecute this cause to its logical conclusion,—the real conservation of our valuable wild life?

/

A Group of Deer

White-tailed does feeding.

CHAPTER VI

PRIVATE GAME PRESERVES AS FACTORS IN CONSERVATION

BY FREDERIC C. WALCOTT[1]

A request from Dr. Hornaday to contribute anything intended to further the protection and propagation of wild life in this country should be taken as a command. When it was suggested that I add a chapter to his Yale lectures to outline the work accomplished by individuals and private associations in establishing game refuges and sanctuaries in the United States, I accepted from sheer enthusiasm for the subject, realizing fully my limitations, but trusting that my brief report on what has been accomplished may inspire similar efforts in others.

A man without a fad is hardly fit for human society. A man with a good wholesome fad often becomes quite independent of the very society which he benefits through his enthusiasm, and there are times when the call from the city to the game preserve is even more imperative, and the problems more absorbing, than those of the farm.

[1] On the subject of this chapter, Mr. Walcott is particularly well fitted to write—by study and research, wide observation, practical experience, and above all, keen interest in, and sympathy for, wild life and its preservation.—W. T. H.

Illustrations from photographs by the author.

Many of our American fads become little less than manias, and all such are quickly dropped. Too much motion is little better than lost motion. The rich man who must live near New York or Boston takes up farming, seriously; and when he has finished fertilizing with gold dollars the sterile acres of his collection of New England deserted farms, he has paid the price of the richest farm or fruit land in California, and he has very little in the end. The moment the golden stream ceases to flow his land reverts to steeplebush, hardhack, gray birch and sumac. Much of this land is admirably suited for wild life and, if left alone, or encouraged in its wild habit, will generously do its share toward protecting and increasing the wild game of this and of other countries, for the ultimate benefit of mankind. Let us then consider the state and private game preserve as a means of increasing our wild life, our food supply, and at the same time utilizing waste places that now are of little value to anyone.

Take the state of Connecticut as an example. Although situated in the center of the most populous district of the United States, with an area of approximately three million acres, about one-third of this, or one million acres, is utterly unsuited for agricultural purposes. It is either marshland, second-growth hardwood, or rough, wild pasture. Massachusetts, Vermont and New Hampshire have many areas of the same general character—thickly populated, but dotted everywhere with deserted farms and waste acres.

State Game Preserves.—Comparatively few of our states have made any effort at the systematic propagation and preservation of game, and fewer still, it would seem, have accurate records of the amount of land within their borders devoted to private preserves. There is still less information regarding the acreage wholly unsuitable for agricultural purposes, that might be devoted to state game preserves. With a view to beginning a permanent record of such statistics, the American Game Protective Association some months ago sent out to the authorities of each state cards containing a list of questions.

The responses were far from satisfactory, both in the number of replies received, and in the amount of information contained therein. That was, however, at least the beginning of an important and necessary work. The returns received show that California, Connecticut, Delaware, Iowa, Kentucky, Missouri, New Jersey, New York and West Virginia have state game-farms, and that on these the species of birds most successfully reared is the ring-necked pheasant. Other game species mentioned are wild turkey, valley quail, Hungarian partridge, Mexican quail, bob-whites, Canadian geese, mallard and black duck, wood-duck, golden and silver pheasant, rabbit, elk and deer.

In California, since the establishment of the game-farm, 4,097 ring-necked pheasants have been distributed, 1,053 wild turkeys, 450 pheasant eggs and 884 turkey eggs. Iowa has distributed 700 ring-necked pheasants. Connecticut has distributed 400, but in the present season (1914) she has raised 6,000 of these birds. So far the output of New Jersey's game-farm is 3,500 pheasants, and it is encouraging to note that in its first year this farm succeeded in raising (under the general supervision of Commissioner Ernest Napier) 4,400 ringnecks, 400 quail, 35 wild turkeys, 5 Canadian geese, 180 mallards and 20 deer. New York's farm so far has stocked that state with 10,000 ring-necked pheasants and distributed 45,500 eggs; while West Virginia has produced 200 ringnecks, 100 Hungarian quail and 3,000 ringneck eggs.

All of the states agree that the propagation methods adopted are increasing the visible supply of game, and several suggest an increase in the number of private preserves to reinforce the game-breeding. Many officials complain that the space allowed for propagating purposes is too limited.

E. C. Hinshaw, state fish and game warden of Iowa, in his reply says: "I am at this time establishing game reserves in every county throughout the state, wherein no hunting will be allowed for five years. All birds liberated will be placed in them, and given every possible protection from hunters and vermin, and will also be provided with food and shelter if necessary, during extremely hard weather."

The State Board of Fisheries and Game at Hart-

FEEDING THE WILD GEESE

Canada geese, that breed each year, eating from the gamekeeper's hands.

ford, Connecticut, declares that dogs should not be allowed to roam at will during the breeding season, and that cats, when found at large, should be treated as vermin. It also contends that the destruction of certain hawks should be encouraged; with which all bird-protectors will agree.

Pitfalls of which the beginner in game-breeding is warned are: overcrowding and its resultant disease, black-head, quail disease, roup, gapes, egg-eating by adult birds, vermin (if eggs are hatched by hens), inadequate regulation of temperature and moisture in incubators, destruction of young birds by rats, unsanitary conditions generally, failure to provide fresh ground in breeding, and predatory foxes.

Information as to the space available for game preserves, or even the area now actually used as such, is difficult to obtain. California tells us it has nearly 2,000 square miles, or 1,280,000 acres, of fresh-water ponds and lakes, and nearly 1,000 miles of coast-line. In addition to the above, it has nearly 2,000 square miles of preserves. Connecticut has 50,000 acres, including private and public lands. Add a generous approximate acreage from several of the other states interested in propagation, and the total, when compared with the acreage of the United States, is relatively insignificant, compared to even a partial list of Scottish moorlands advertised in the London *Times* of July 3, 1914, for lease during this shooting season—a total of 29 moors aggregating 235,000 acres, with a season's yield of 13,500 brace of grouse and 287 stags, together with several miles of trout and salmon streams.

If the states that already show a healthy interest in the better protection of their game should now throw into service the unused acreage they well could spare, we would have breeding-grounds in comparison with which even these of Europe would seem small. Here is a list of available lands which experts estimate certain states could afford to use for game propagation on a commercial basis:

Connecticut	1,000,000 acres.
New Jersey	2,007,000 acres.
West Virginia . . .	10,000,000 acres.
Utah	28,320 square miles.
South Dakota . . .	15,000,000 acres.
New Mexico	2,000,000 acres.
(Already preserved for private use.)	
Montana	25,000,000 acres.
Minnesota	7,000,000 acres.
Maine	5,000,000 acres.
Georgia	500,000 acres.

New York contains 800,000 acres already in private preserves in the Adirondacks alone, and a much larger area is owned and controlled by the state.

Nearly every state has a forest, fish and game commission, some of the states have park commissions, and all of the eastern states have boards of education. Clearly, it seems to be the duty of these

boards and commissions to coöperate in utilizing
these wild lands for the benefit of the people at
large. This is to be accomplished by reforestation,
to protect the water supply; by stocking the woods
and water with intelligently selected birds, mammals and fish; and by building state roads to and
through reserved tracts, that they may become
accessible as free camp-sites and pleasure resorts to
conserve the health of the people and supply
another source of healthful pleasure and recreation
for those with moderate incomes.

We must not forget what has been done and is
being done in this direction. It is important that
all the departments of conservation should work in
the closest harmony with each other, to prevent
duplication of investment and labor. Even though
the conservation laws of many states are in urgent
need of reform, still we have made, and are making,
marked progress.

If space permitted, it would be interesting and
helpful to discuss the methods employed on the various game-farms, and analyze the results of game-
distribution in each state; but the chief purpose of
this article is to appeal to the imagination of the
man who, as owner of a large or small tract of
semi-wild land, should be contributing substan-
tially toward the increase of the supply of wild life
that in general is so rapidly vanishing. Although
the work done by some of the states is already

important, it should be supplemented by the owners of private preserves.

There is little danger that we in the United States will fall into the error that England has made in allowing three-fourths of her land to be owned by one-fourth of her population. Neither is it likely that we shall become a nation of sportsmen to the same extent that the English have. But if by state and individual effort we can, in the next generation or two, increase our song-birds, our game-birds and water-fowl, as has been done in England, the economic results to the consumers of farm products, in the lower prices of game food and the love of nature that must accompany an interest in and knowledge of these things, will prove among our important national assets.

The Beginning of Private Game Preserves in America.—From the earliest colonial times there have been game preserves in this country, both of the fenced and unfenced types; and there are records of estates attempting to stock with English pheasants, European gray and red-legged partridges, extending back more than a hundred years. Perhaps the most interesting among the early game preserves was Bohemia Manor in Cecil County, Maryland, where Augustine Hermann established, in 1661, a walled deer-park of considerable size. The game preserves of the early period were found chiefly in Virginia and Maryland, and to a lesser extent in the Atlantic States to the south and north, where the English royalists and other wealthy foreigners had founded estates. There were no early game preserves in New England, doubtless owing to the temper of the colonists.

The Atlantic coast from New Jersey southward was originally the best preserved section of America. As a matter of custom the farmers and planters of the southern states have reserved the shooting on their lands for themselves and their friends, and that system still is in vogue, except that in many instances the owners of the lands have leased the shooting rights to wealthy sportsmen. In the Carolinas, for example, hundreds of thousands of acres of quail lands are leased to individuals and clubs, a large part of whose membership is drawn from the northern and western states. Clubs and individuals have also acquired the wild-fowl shooting-rights along the bays, sounds and rivers of the Atlantic coast, and to an equal extent the best localities on the Pacific coast, chiefly in the great state of California. Along the northern border of the United States, particularly on the Great Lakes, many of the best wild-fowl marshes are similarly controlled, and there has also been extensive development of preserves for the shooting of wild fowl throughout the Mississippi River states and westward to the Pacific coast.

Important Private Game Preserves in the United States.—In 1858 Judge John Dean Caton, who subsequently wrote an authoritative work on

"The Antelope and Deer of America," established a deer park near Ottawa, Illinois. Here Judge Caton made a highly valuable study of American big game in captivity.

In 1886 the late Austin Corbin began fencing in his game park near Newport, New Hampshire, including within it the farm which had been his boyhood home. This park is the largest private fenced preserve in America, containing within its area about 27,000 acres of wooded upland country diversified by occasional cleared areas which once were hill farms. It is estimated that there have been as many as 4,000 big game animals in this park at one time, including buffalo, wapiti, deer and wild boars. The native white-tailed deer are naturally the most numerous.

Blue Mountain Forest Park, as it is called, was established as a hunting-preserve. It has had the good fortune to have associated with it, for several years, the New Hampshire naturalist, Ernest Harold Baynes, with whose interesting studies the public is familiar through his published articles.

The largest fenced preserve in New York State is the park owned by Edward H. Litchfield of Brooklyn, near Tupper Lake, in the Adirondacks, which comprises in its area about 10,000 acres. Mr. Litchfield has stocked this preserve with many species of American big game animals, and also wild boar.

Another interesting preserve of this type is that

FIVE O'CLOCK P. M.

Scores of wild black ducks fly in every evening at about five from the other ponds.

of Mr. C. F. Dieterich, who for more than twenty years has had about 3,000 acres under fence at Millbrook, Dutchess County, New York. Mr. Dieterich successfully introduced German hares and has also made interesting experiments with roe deer, which now seem thoroughly acclimatized.

Mr. Chester W. Chapin's preserve is in Sullivan County, New York. The late Dr. W. Seward Webb had a large tract of forest land fenced at his Nehasane Park in the Adirondacks. William Rockefeller also experimented with exotic deer at his Bay Pond preserve in the Adirondacks, and George J. Gould at one time had a herd of elk at his place near Arkville in the Catskills. As far back as 1902, as a result of a computation made by the State Forest, Fish and Game Commission of New York, there was a total of 791,208 acres of land included in game preserves in the Adirondacks. Most of this land, however, was not fenced, but simply posted by the owners against public shooting, as they desired to have the exclusive privilege of taking the deer, ruffed grouse and trout native to the region.

In recent years a marked development has occurred in a type of preserve where game is not only protected but propagated. It is interesting to note that while many of these preserves are founded for the purpose of sport, there is an appreciable number where scientific or æsthetic objects are the governing factor. One of the first and most noteworthy of the preserves belonging to an incorporated association was that of the Blooming Grove Park Association in Pike County, Pennsylvania, established in 1871, where, in addition to the native grouse and other game-birds, hundreds of pheasants are shot each year by club members. The Clove Valley Rod and Gun Club of Dutchess County, New York, is another successful example of this type. It was the first organization to profit by the new "Bayne law," providing for the sale of mallard ducks reared in captivity, and marketed according to law. In 1912 this club reared and marketed about 4,000 mallards, at a net profit of approximately $2,500.

One of the earliest attempts at systematic propagation of game-birds in this country was made by Mr. Rutherford Stuyvesant in 1887, at his place called "Tranquillity," in Allamuchy, Warren County, New Jersey. Mr. Stuyvesant's preserve consisted of 8,000 acres, and his success was very largely due to the expert assistants he secured from Scotland. A brief review of the work accomplished by Mr. Stuyvesant will be interesting, as he was in a sense a pioneer in this country in systematic game-bird rearing.

Donald McVicar, who had been head gamekeeper for the Duke of Leinster, Kildare, Ireland, in 1887 brought over from England for Mr. Stuyvesant 500 ring-necked pheasant eggs. From these he reared only about 70 birds. Eggs are quite apt to be rendered infertile by shipping long distances. The second season 65 live birds were brought over from England for breeding stock. In a few seasons the annual hatch was brought up to about 4,000 pheasants. One year 500 live quail were brought from the South, and set out in the fall in small wire coops. They were fed regularly and wintered well, and in the spring they were liberated. A great many birds were reared by this stock, but practically all of them left "Tranquillity" before the next winter.

In 1891 part of the preserve was enclosed for deer, white-tailed, mule and wapiti, which were liberated and did well for several years.

An experiment was made of crossing American bison bulls with Galloway cows; but nineteen cows died calving, and the experiment was given up.

In the early nineties a beaver colony was started, which proved successful. The offspring of this colony are now breeding in open territory in New York State, without adequate protection.

The ruffed grouse, native to the Tranquillity district, increased rapidly on account of the persistent trapping of vermin, and the ring-necked pheasants apparently did not molest them or diminish their numbers. The ring-necked pheasants keep to the open woods and fields, and to some extent apparently drive the grouse deeper into the woods, but beyond this do not interfere with them.

One of the most important contributions of this

preserve has proved to be the men that McVicar brought over with him, Adam Scott, Duncan Dunn, Donald Monroe, Neal Clark, and his son, A. G. McVicar, all from Inveraray, Argyleshire, Scotland. These men have greatly advanced the development of private preserves in eastern United States.

In Canada, the Province of Quebec has adopted a system of leasing crown lands that has resulted in the creation of a number of large shooting and fishing preserves. The provincial law limits to 200 square miles the extent of territory that may be held by any one club, and three dollars per square mile per annum is the minimum price charged for shooting privileges. The Megantic Club, which owns or controls 125,000 acres of land partly in Quebec and partly in Maine, is one of the oldest and most representative clubs of this type.

Charles C. Worthington of New Jersey has for many years maintained one of the largest and most successful bird refuges in the country and has recently offered his 80,000-acre tract to the state of New Jersey to be held by the state as a permanent game refuge. He has been so successful in breeding white-tailed deer that at one time he reported a surplus of about 1,000 head.

Another notable instance of bird protection and propagation is Mr. Henry Ford's 2,100-acre farm and bird sanctuary near Detroit, Michigan. Mr. Ford has encouraged the "farmers' best friends" to

Winter Quarters

Rat and weasel proof winter quarters for the pheasants that are caught up in October as breeding stock the next spring.

help him by setting out shrubs and erecting nesting boxes in every spot congenial to the birds. He is one of the most efficient enthusiasts in conserving bird life in order to lessen the damage to crops by insects, which the United States Department of Agriculture estimates amounts to $800,000,000 annually. He entered very actively into the campaign for the passage of the federal migratory bird law, and he is one of the founders of Dr. Hornaday's Permanent Wild Life Protection Fund.

The experiment station of the American Game Protective and Propagation Association is at South Carver, Cape Cod, Massachusetts. The preserve contains 6,000 acres of land, including sixteen fresh-water ponds, where deer, ring-necked pheasants, mallard, wood-duck, quail and ruffed grouse are being reared for distribution among the members of the Association to encourage the extension of private preserves.

The game breeders' association, formerly of Wading River, Long Island, and now at Sparrow-bush, New York, has made extensive experiments with pheasants, ducks and quail. Last season they gathered 4,000 eggs from 170 mallard ducks and hatched 2,500 ducklings.

The Woodmont Rod and Gun Club, in the mountains of the western part of Maryland near Harper's Ferry, has accomplished excellent results in breeding the wild turkey and quail.

Dr. J. W. Whealton, of Chincoteague Island,

Virginia, has probably been more successful in raising Canada geese than anyone else in the United States. He has had much experience in raising water-fowl, is a careful observer and has been most helpful in advising beginners.

In 1913 Mrs. Russell Sage purchased, through Messrs. Ward & McIlhenny, the whole of Marsh Island, Louisiana, about 100 miles west of the mouth of the Mississippi. This is one of the most important winter feeding-grounds for water-fowl in the United States, and long has been a favorite resort for market-hunters. Mrs. Sage has offered this great bird sanctuary to the United States Government as a gift, to be kept always as a bird refuge, and in due time it undoubtedly will be accepted. At present it is being guarded at the expense of Mrs. Sage.

An announcement has just been made of a purchase of 85,000 acres of marshland near the mouth of the Mississippi in Louisiana at a cost of approximately $225,000, by the Rockefeller Foundation. Mr. E. A. McIlhenny of Avery Island, Louisiana, brought this tract of land to the attention of the Rockefeller Foundation. The tract is only a few miles from Marsh Island, above referred to, and it is one of the most celebrated winter homes and spring breeding-places for land birds and water-fowl.

Colonel Anthony R. Kuser has maintained for several years at his home in Bernardsville, New

Jersey, a large aviary for pheasants and has successfully reared in captivity a great many different species. Colonel Kuser has always been an enthusiast in game propagation, and in addition to the work he has done for the state and the New York Zoölogical Society, he is now developing a large private game preserve near High Point, New Jersey.

The Audubon Societies of the United States are ably administered by a group of enthusiastic and successful men and women. They have caught the spirit of that pioneer worker, Mr. William Dutcher, who founded the National Association, and they should receive the loyal support of the entire country in their crusade against bird enemies. One of the most destructive of these enemies is the immigrant from Southern Europe, whose Sunday bag is too often filled with our most useful and sweetest songsters.

The most effective remedy is the instruction in natural history by our public schools, which is creating in the minds of our future citizens a realization of the economic and æsthetic value of the birds.

The Ethics of the Aviary.—The love of all wild animals is growing apace in this country, and with it is growing a dislike for everything that is cruel in the confinement or treatment of animals. The indiscriminate keeping of caged wild birds and animals should be discouraged as much as the indiscriminate collecting of eggs and song-birds.

The pinioned caged birds and water-fowl are beautiful things to look at, and the aviary and flying cage are interesting, but the first cost of the plant is large, and often the owner, becoming tired of this form of amusement, or disgusted with the sight of wild birds closely confined in unnatural surroundings, decides to give his pets the freedom they long for, or confine his efforts to only such varieties as may be liberated, or raised in a state of semi-domestication.

The zoölogical societies should carry on experiments in propagation, where the results can be carefully tabulated and made available for the public.

Wherever anyone feels disposed to maintain a private aviary and permit the public to view the collection upon stated occasions, it becomes an important adjunct to the education of the public. This method has been initiated with conspicuous generosity and success by Mrs. Frederic Ferris Thompson with her extensive aviary at her country home, "Sonneberg," in the suburbs of Canandaigua, New York.

The tendency even in the zoölogical parks is, or should be, to get away as far as possible from artificial conditions of life, by building large flying cages, large runways for the animals, and letting as many species as possible fly or roam at large within the main enclosures.

The zoölogical societies of this country should

BY THE BROOK'S EDGE

Gray and black mallards, red-heads, canvasbacks, wood and mandarin ducks, pin-tails, snow, Hutchins, cackling and Canada geese wintering by the edge of a spring-fed brook to the left of the picture.

coöperate to the fullest extent with the state and private preserves to encourage their development, and furnish, practically at cost for services and expenses, a consulting expert to enable the beginner to start intelligently, avoid serious mistakes, correct unavoidable errors, prescribe against sickness and help enforce sanitary conditions by emphasizing at all times the importance of the great cardinal principle, hygiene.   The New York Zoölogical Society is already doing much along this line.

The Response of Wild Fowl to Man's Protection.—It is far more interesting to tame a wild bird by coaxing it to feed on your window-sill every morning than it is to look after a thrush that is eating his heart out in a small cage as he watches through the bars of his prison the chickadees on the window-sill.

It is this growing—not humanizing, but *animalizing*—instinct that is turning us with something akin to disgust away from the ill-smelling, poorly kept cage collections of the often misguided individual enthusiast to the free out-of-door range, where the birds that have been migrating over those acres for countless generations are glad to drop down out of the sky and feed, eager to accept protection from their most deadly enemy, man.

Practical Suggestions.—It is astonishing what can be accomplished in two or three seasons from the smallest beginning, provided a few fundamentals are observed.   A successful game preserve and

bird refuge can be made on almost any land
unsuited to agricultural purposes, that is partially
covered with trees, either virgin forest or second-
growth hardwood, or wild pasture overgrown with
bushes and containing some fresh water, preferably
a stream with pools or small ponds, and situated in
the vicinity of a river running north and south, the
favorite route of migratory birds.   These conditions can be found almost anywhere in New England, in any of the states on the Atlantic coast and
in many states bordering large rivers, such as the
Hudson, Savannah, Potomac, Mississippi, Missouri, Rio Grande or Sacramento.   They are also
to be found in many portions of our very extensive
lake frontage.   A wooded island is of course ideal,
because on such areas the vermin pest can be so
easily controlled.   The following table illustrates
the marked effect of systematic killing of vermin
at a private preserve in England:

VERMIN

(Killed between the seasons of 1903 and 1904.)

Rats	5,959
Stoats	270
Weasels	271
Hedgehogs	541
Rooks	304
Jays	364
Magpies	2
Jackdaws	39
Cats	154
	7,904

GAME

	1903	1904
Pheasants	943	1,509
Partridges	790	4,774
Woodcock	19	27
Hare	462	2,236
Snipe	3	1
Wood-ducks (Mallard) .	12	
Pigeons	5	38
Deer	46	
Fawns	30	
Wild sheep	2	
Peacocks	1	
Rabbits	15,346	18,519

Increase chiefly due to trapping of vermin.
Bounty of 1 penny per rat to everyone except keepers.

This record was made on a leased preserve after the place had been neglected for several seasons.

The most marked increases occur in the partridge and hare, which are not raised by hand, showing that the increase is chiefly due to the reduction of vermin.

There is a fascination about letting semi-wild land slowly and methodically revert to its original state, and in encouraging one's land to respond to the call of the wild. It costs only a small portion of the amount required to run a farm, it has fewer worries, and the making of a preserve for birds, water-fowl or mammals, whether it is to be a refuge for song-birds, as all preserves become willy-nilly, or to supply the market with game at the prevailing fancy prices as a reasonably lucrative enterprise, is interesting and satisfying beyond all description.

The readiness of nearly all wild animals to accept man's proposals to protect and partially feed them is amazing. It appeals wonderfully to one's sense of fair play to find a flock of wild geese meeting you more than half-way by staying with you and rearing their brood as long as you give them a little corn at the same time each day; and the knowledge that your own wild ducks decline to go south, when literally thousands of their wilder friends come and go each spring and fall, warms the cockles of your heart.

As an illustration of the intelligence of wild water-fowl and the quickness with which they learn to take advantage of protection that is offered, I might cite an incident that was told me by that keen sportsman and ardent lover of wild life, Lord William Percy.

It seems that in the north of England, not far from Alnwick Castle, Lord William's home, lives a gentleman named Grant, who while offering every protection to all wild fowl on his place never has allowed any shooting. A flock of wild gray mallards came annually to Mr. Grant's place, and as they were never molested they became as tame as barnyard fowl, and would come to the kitchen door to be fed. In the open, however, these birds were even more shy than ordinary wild fowl, and Lord William stated that the professional gunners came to know this flock, which gradually increased to four or five hundred, on account of their wariness and would make no attempt either to stalk or decoy them in their flight up and down the coast.

Description of the Author's Game Preserve at Norfolk, Connecticut.—A brief description of a preserve of 4,000 acres started three years ago by Mr. S. W. Childs and the writer in the northwestern part of Connecticut may be of interest, to show how quickly wild life responds to protection, and to indicate some of the stumbling-blocks and cardinal principles in the making of a preserve.

As I sit here writing on the porch of a house overlooking a typical Connecticut pond about three-quarters of a mile long and half a mile wide, a poodle pointer imported from Germany and an English setter are standing by my side, quivering with excitement as they watch eight ring-necked pheasants feeding on a small piece of lawn a few feet away.

Canada geese are making a great uproar by the shore of the pond below as they chase back and forth, flapping their wings, apparently trying to encourage their goslings, now at the end of August nearly full grown, to rise and fly.

Wild black mallards and wood-ducks that bred this year on the place, and several hundred hand-reared gray mallards, all able to fly, are to be seen in the air and on the water, and a herd of fifteen native Connecticut white-tailed deer, with four

fawns born this spring, instead of the cows that
have called that ground their home for the last fifty
years, are browsing in sight of the house, among
some young white birches that are growing in a
typical wild pasture lot of about seventy-five acres.

There are three other ponds on this place, and
last spring several broods of black ducks were
reared on each. Two of the ponds are natural
water-holes, and the other two are artificial. The
former were reclaimed by putting in small stone
dams where the weather of years had destroyed the
handicraft of pioneer lumbermen. The latter are
streams dammed at points where narrow breaks in
the ground permitted of short, inexpensive timber
and earth structures.

Between two and three thousand black ducks
drop into the home pond each fall and remain until
late December before going farther south; and each
fall and spring, from forty to fifty wild Canada
geese stay with our geese several days, for food. A
snow goose caught in a fish net on Long Island
Sound last fall, and sent to us after being wing-
clipped, has become perfectly tame, and is now
flying about as naturally as she did in the wild
state. A wing-tipped cackling goose, wounded at
Horn Point, Virginia, near Currituck Sound (the
only record of this bird on the Atlantic coast), was
brought to the preserve in January, 1913, and
liberated. The broken wing soon healed, allowing
her to fly perfectly, and this bird has twice declined

THE HOME POND

Ducks and geese on the edge of the home pond.

to migrate with the larger wild flock. She has mated with a Hutchins gander, and has succeeded with her charms in enticing a Canadian gander from his mate, to whom he had been faithful for eight years!

We have liberated between 800 and 1,000 ring-necked pheasants of our own raising each season, and now expect to raise from 1,500 to 2,000 gray mallards every season, for the market. Gray mallards bring in the market from $3 to $3.50 per pair and it costs from 75 cents to $1 to bring a mallard to maturity. The eggs sell at from $15 to $20 per hundred.

Pheasants are much more difficult to raise than ducks, but enough could be sold each year to decrease materially the cost of running the pre-serve, provided the law of the state in which the birds are raised permits the sale of hand-reared game. The New York state law is excellent in this respect, and other states should allow the sale of hand-reared game, in order to encourage their increase by artificial methods and create a new industry.

The overflow from private preserves nearly always stocks the neighboring woods and fields, affording excellent sport. The pheasant is largely an insectivorous bird, preferring the open field and the edge of the wooded areas to the dense woods, and probably interferes very little with our native ruffed grouse. He wanders far afield, however, and unless the land round about is suited to him, he will leave for the more congenial environment of the river bottom and the low-lying farms.

One of the great desiderata for American game-rearing is a manual of instruction adapted to climatic conditions as found between Virginia to the south and New Hampshire to the north. Such a manual, to be really useful, must be written by a man who has had a long and successful experience; and when such a manual is written, it will give a tremendous impetus to game propagation. It must cover the following subjects: 1. Selection of a preserve for birds and mammals. 2. Exterminating vermin, such as the bay lynx or bobcat, skunk, fox, weasel, domestic cat, rat, crow, red squirrel, great horned owl, sharp-shinned and Cooper's hawk. 3. Natural foods for pheasants, quail, grouse and surface-feeding ducks; methods and conditions for planting. 4. The care of adult birds, with formulæ and regulations for feeding. 5. The care and feeding of the young. 6. The management and feeding of deer.

The Commercial Side of Breeding Game in Captivity.—The private game preserve and bird sanctuary under reasonable regulations should be encouraged in every way by the states for the following reasons:

1.   To supplement the work now being done by many of the states and to create a large overflow for the benefit of the people at large.

2. To increase the insectivorous birds, whose economic value has been so convincingly set forth by Mr. E. H. Forbush in his book, "Useful Birds and Their Protection."

3. To increase the supply of meat and thus bring it within the reach of more people. The comparative prices of game between this country and England during the last century reveal the rapidity with which our wild life is vanishing.

EXCERPT FROM "THE GAME MARKET OF TO-DAY," HENRY OLDYS, UNITED STATES DEPARTMENT OF AGRICULTURE, 1910

	New York, 1763	New York, 1910	London, 1910
Partridge,[1] each,	$.24	$1.75 -2.00	$.16-.25
Grouse,[2] each,	.30	1.50	.24-.36
Mallard, each,	.25	.62½	.24-.36
Teal, each,	.12	.37½- .50	.16-.24
Snipe, per dozen,	.30	2.00 -3.00	.08-.16
Quail, per dozen,		3.00 -4.50	

Ring-necked pheasant, New York, 1913, wholesale $4 to $4.50 per pair.
Ring-necked pheasant, London, 1913, wholesale $1 per pair.
1653—Whole deer $1.20.
1765—Whole deer 17.50 (maximum price).
1910—Whole deer 43.73 (maximum price wholesale).

4. To add interest to the reclamation and reforestation of practically worthless acres which

[1] Probably means ruffed grouse in New York.
[2] Heath-hen in New York markets in 1763; in 1910 this would be ruffed grouse.

should be exempt from taxation while being improved, under the German system of taxing the crop after the improvements have been completed and lumbering begins.

In short, the salvation of our wild life that is so rapidly vanishing can only be accomplished by the game farm and the game refuge, state and private; and everyone owning even a small tract of semi-wild land should help the cause of conservation.

Let each one do his share to restore the balance which man has so rudely and persistently upset. Man ruthlessly destroyed the larger carnivora until the smaller species, less useful and less dangerous to him, increased abnormally, thereby destroying the bird life so essential in keeping in check the insect life. If we reduce the number of small carnivora to normal, the bird life will quickly respond, the injurious insect life will promptly decrease and useful vegetation will increase correspondingly.

Let the waste areas be peopled with the animal and bird life of a hundred years ago. Let the forests, now still, echo with the whistle of the deer and the bugle of the elk, our waterways answer to the honk of the wild goose, and our farms will resound to the chorus of myriads of song-birds! Then, when the "red gods call," we can go; and we shall be a stronger, hardier, better race through our appreciation and enjoyment of the wild life we have helped to reinstate.

A BIBLIOGRAPHY OF MORE RECENT WORKS ON WILD BIRDS, WITH SPECIAL REFERENCE TO GAME PRESERVES AND THE PROTECTION AND PROPAGATION OF GAME

BY FREDERIC C. WALCOTT

In a general way I have tried in compiling this bibliography to include only the more recent works, and works that are not restricted in the ground they cover to any small section of territory or limited number of species. Where exception has been made to these two principles, I have felt that there was justification.

The books are classified by countries. Capital letters following certain titles indicate call number of books at New York Public Library.

THE WORLD

Four Centuries of Legislation on Birds. W. G. Clarke. Antiquary, London, 1909. C. A.

ENGLAND

A Gamekeeper's Note Book. Owen Jones and Marcus Woodward. E. Arnold, London, 1910. M. Y. O.

Birds and the Plumage Trade. S. L. Bensusan. Nineteenth Century, London, 1913. D. A.

The Migration of Birds. T. A. Coward. University Press, Cambridge, 1912. Q. M. E.

Aviaries and Aviary Life. Wesley T. Page. The Avian
    Press, Ashbourne, 1912.
A History of Fowling. H. A. MacPherson. David Douglas,
    Edinburgh, 1897.
The Solution of the Mystery of Bird Flight. George L. O.
    Davidson. Nineteenth Century and After, London, 1912.
    D. A.
Lost and Vanishing Birds. C. Dixon. J. MacQueen,
    London, 1898. Q. M. D.
The Complete Wildfowler. Stanley Duncan and G. Thorne.
    G. Richards, Ltd., London, 1912. M. Y. T.
Studies in Bird Migration. Wm. Eagle Clarke. Gurney &
    Jackson, London, 1912. Q. M. E.
The Flight of Birds. F. W. Headley. Witherby & Co.,
    London, 1912. Q. M. D.
The Brent Valley Bird Sanctuary. W. M. Webb. Selborne
    Society, Brent Valley, England, 1911. Q. M. D.
British Diving Ducks. J. G. Millais. Longmans, Green &
    Co., New York, 1913.
Natural History of the British Surface-Feeding Ducks. J. G.
    Millais. Longmans, Green & Co., 1902.
The Natural History of British Game Birds. J. G. Millais.
    Longmans, Green & Co., 1909.
The Mammals of Great Britain and Ireland. J. G. Millais.
    Longmans, Green & Co., 1904.

NORTH AMERICA

The American Natural History. W. T. Hornaday. Fireside
    Edition, 1914. Charles Scribner's Sons, New York.
Color Key to North American Birds. F. M. Chapman.
    American Museum Natural History, New York, 1903.
Key to North American Birds. Elliott Coues. Dana Estes &
    Co., Boston, 1903.
The Bird. C. William Beebe. Henry Holt & Co., New
    York, 1906.

Distribution and Migration of North American Shorebirds. Wells W. Cooke. Government Printing Office, Washington, 1912. Q. G. S.

Chronology and Index of the More Important Events in American Game Protection, 1776-1911. T. S. Palmer. Government Printing Office, Washington, 1912. Q. G. S.

North American Birds Eggs. C. S. Reed. Many illustrations. 1904.

EASTERN NORTH AMERICA

Handbook of Birds of Eastern North America. F. M. Chapman. D. Appleton & Co., New York, 1895. Q. M. Q.

GREENLAND

Die Vögel der Arktik. Band IV, Lieferung 1, pp. 81-288. Gustav Fischer, Jena, 1904. A detailed synopsis of Arctic bird life.

CANADA—*General*

Catalogue of Canadian Birds, giving their nesting habits. J. and J. M. Macoun. Government Printing Bureau, Ottawa, 1909.

CANADA—*Provinces*

Labrador.—Birds of Labrador. C. M. Townsend and G. M. Allen. Proceedings, Boston Society of Natural History, XXXIII, pp. 277-428. 1907.

Manitoba.—Fauna of Manitoba. E. T. Seton. British Association Handbook, Winnipeg, 1909.

Ontario.—Check List of the Birds of Ontario. Warwick, Beas & Rutter, Toronto, 1900.

UNITED STATES—*General*

The Destruction of our Birds and Mammals. W. T. Hornaday. New York Zoölogical Society, 1898.

Migratory Movements of Birds in Relation to Weather. W. W. Cooke. Government Printing Office, Washington, 1911. Q. M. D.

Economic Value of Predaceous Birds and Mammals. A. C. Fisher. Government Printing Office, Washington, 1909. V. P. E.

American Game Bird Shooting. George Bird Grinnell. Forest and Stream Publishing Co., New York, 1910. M. Y. T.

Birds of Town and Country. H. W. Henshaw. National Geographic Magazine, Washington, D. C., 1914. K. A. A.

The Policeman of the Air: An Account of the Biological Survey of the United States Department of Agriculture. H. W. Henshaw. National Geographic Magazine, vol. 19, pp. 29-118, Washington, 1909.

Our Vanishing Wild Life. W. T. Hornaday. New York Zoölogical Society and Charles Scribner's Sons, New York, 1913. M. Y. D.

Game Bird Enemies. D. W. Huntington. Independent, vol. 64, p. 500, New York, 1908. D. A.

The Sport of Bird Study. H. K. Job. Outing Press, New York, 1908.

Birds as Weed Destroyers. S. D. Judd. Year Book, United States Department of Agriculture, 1898.

Encouraging Birds Around the Home. Frederick H. Kennard. National Geographic Magazine, vol. 25, pp. 315-344, Washington, 1914.

Raising Deer and Other Large Game Animals in the United States. David E. Lantz. United States Department of Agriculture, Washington, 1910.

Five Important Wild Duck Foods. W. L. McAtee. United States Department of Agriculture, 1914.

Our Vanishing Shorebirds. W. L. McAtee. United States Biological Survey, Circular 79. Q. G. S.

Plants Useful to Attract Birds and Protect Fruit. W. L.
McAtee. Year Book, United States Department of Agriculture, 1909. Q. E. I.

The Game Market of To-day. Henry Oldys. Government
Printing Office, Washington, 1911. V. T. B.

Directory of Officials and Organizations concerned with the
Protection of Birds and Game. United States Bureau of
Biological Survey, 1913. Q. M. I.

Importation of Game Birds and Geese for Propagation. T. S.
Palmer and Henry Oldys. United States Department of
Agriculture, Washington, 1904.

Methods of Attracting Birds. Gilbert H. Trafton. Houghton
Mifflin Co., Boston, 1910. Q. M. I.

National Reservations for the Protection of Wild Life. T. S.
Palmer. Government Printing Office, Washington, 1912.
Q. G. S.

Private Game Preserves and Their Future in the United States.
T. S. Palmer. Government Printing Office, Washington,
1910. Q. G. S.

Progress of Game Protection. T. S. Palmer. United States
Biological Survey, 1910. Q. G. S.

Revealing and Concealing Coloration in Birds and Mammals.
Theodore Roosevelt. American Museum Natural History,
New York, 1911. P. Q. A.

How to Destroy Rats. David E. Lantz. United States
Department of Agriculture, Bulletin No. 369, September
3, 1909.

Birds That Hunt and Are Hunted. Neltje Blanchan. Double-
day, Page & Co., New York.

Among the Water Fowl. H. K. Job.

Wild Ducks. Capt. W. C. Oates.

Fox Trapping. A. R. Harding.

Ornamental Water Fowl. Hon. Rose Hubbard.

Saving the Ducks and Geese. Wells W. Cooke. National
Geographic Magazine, March, 1913.

UNITED STATES—*Sections*

Mississippi Valley.—Report on Bird Migration in the Mississippi Valley in the Years 1884 and 1885. W. W. Cooke. Bulletin No. 2, Division Economic Ornithology, United States Biological Survey, Washington.

New England.—History of the Game Birds, Wild-fowl and Shore Birds of Massachusetts and Adjacent States, with Observations on Their Recent Decrease, Also Means for Conserving Those Still in Existence. E. H. Forbush. Massachusetts Board of Agriculture, Boston, 1912.

Pacific Coast.—Game Birds and Game Fishes of the Pacific Coast. H. T. Payne. Newspaper Publishing Co., Los Angeles, Calif., 1913. Q. M. D.

Southeast.—Birds Known to Eat the Boll Weevil. Vernon Bailey. Government Printing Office, Washington, 1905. Q. G. S.

MISCELLANEOUS STATES

Alaska.—National Bird and Mammal Reservations in Alaska in Charge of the United States Department of Agriculture. Circular 71. Washington, 1910. Q. G. S.

Colorado.—The Practical Value of Birds. Junius Henderson. University of Colorado, University Extension, Division Natural History, Series No. 1, Boulder, Colo., 1913. P. Q. A.

Massachusetts.—Special Report on Decrease of Certain Birds and Its Causes, with Suggestions for Bird Protection. E. H. Forbush. Massachusetts State Board of Agriculture, Boston, 1908.

Useful Birds and Their Protection, 1907. E. H. Forbush.

New York.—The Economic Preservation of Birds. S. L. Bensusan. Contemporary Review, New York, 1914. D. A.

The Economic Value of Birds to the State. F. M. Chapman.
New York State Forest, Fish and Game Commission,
Albany, 1903. Q. M. I.

Birds of New York. Elon Howard Eaton. New York State
Education Department, Albany, 1910.

Birds in Relation to Agriculture. F. H. Hall. New York
State Agricultural Department, Circular 56. J. B. Lyon
& Co., Albany, 1912. V. P. Z.

Ohio.—Effect on Birds of Establishment of Park and Reser-
voirs at Youngstown, Ohio. George L. Fordyce. Wilson
Bulletin, Chicago, 1914. Q. M. A.

Oregon.—Some Common Birds of Oregon with Notes as to
Their Economic Relation to Man. W. L. Finley. N. S.
Duniway, Salem, 1908. Q. M. Q.

Pennsylvania.—Recommendations as to Trapping and Care
of Quail. Use of Poison for Vermin and Crows. Joseph
Kalbfus. Harrisburg Publishing Co., Harrisburg, Pa.,
1908. Q. M. I.

Wisconsin.—Anon the Reasons for Bird Migration: A Favorite
Food Theory. A. C. Burrill. Bulletin Wisconsin Natural
History Society, Milwaukee, 1912. P. Q. A.

GERMANY

Sanctuaries for Birds on German Coasts. Selborne Magazine,
vol. 24, pp. 45-49, London, 1913. M. S. Y.

How to Attract and Protect Wild Birds. Martin Hiesemann.
Witherby & Co., London, 1911.

INDEX

Use and Abuse
of
America's Natural Resources

An Arno Press Collection

Ayres, Quincy Claude. **Soil Erosion and Its Control.** 1936

Barger, Harold and Sam H. Schurr. **The Mining Industries, 1899–1939.** 1944

Carman, Harry J., editor. **Jesse Buel:** Agricultural Reformer. 1947

Circular from the General Land Office Showing the Manner of Proceeding to Obtain Title to Public Lands. 1899

Fernow, Bernhard E. **Economics of Forestry.** 1902

Gannett, Henry, editor. **Report of the National Conservation Commission, February 1909.** Three volumes. 1909

Giddens, Paul H. **The Birth of the Oil Industry.** 1938

Greeley, William B. **Forests and Men.** 1951

Hornaday, William T. **Wild Life Conservation in Theory and Practice.** 1914

Ise, John. **The United States Forest Policy.** 1920

Ise, John. **The United States Oil Policy.** 1928

James, Harlean. **Romance of the National Parks.** 1939

Kemper, J. P. **Rebellious River.** 1949

Kinney, J. P **The Development of Forest Law in America.** *Including,* Forest Legislation in America Prior to March 4, 1789. 1917

Larson, Agnes M. **History of the White Pine Industry in Minnesota.** 1949

Liebig, Justus, von. **The Natural Lawss of Husbandry.** 1863

Lindley, Curtis H. **A Treatise on the American Law Relating to Mines and Mineral Lands.** Two volumes. 2nd edition. 1903

Lokken, Roscoe L. **Iowa**—Public Land Disposal. 1942

McGee, W. J., editor. **Proceedings of a Conference of Governors in the White House, May 13–15, 1908.** 1909

Mead, Elwood. **Irrigation Institutions.** 1903

Moreell, Ben. **Our Nation's Water Resources**—Policies and Politics. 1956

Murphy, Blakely M., editor. **Conservation of Oil & Gas: A Legal History, 1948.** 1949

Newell, Frederick Haynes. **Water Resources:** Present and Future Uses. 1920.

Nimmo, Joseph, Jr. **Report in Regard to the Range and Ranch Cattle Business of the United States.** 1885

Nixon, Edgar B., editor. **Franklin D. Roosevelt & Conservation, 1911–1945.** Two volumes. 1957

Peffer, E. Louise. **The Closing of the Public Domain.** 1951

Preliminary Report of the Inland Waterways Commission. 60th Congress, 1st Session, Senate Document No. 325. 1908

Puter, S. A. D. & Horace Stevens. **Looters of the Public Domain.** 1908

Record, Samuel J. & Robert W. Hess. **Timbers of the New World.** 1943

Report of the Public Lands Commission, with Appendix. 58th Congress, 3d Session, Senate Document No. 189. 1905

Report of the Public Lands Commission, Created by the Act of March 3, 1879. 46th Congress, 2d Session, House of Representatives Ex. Doc. No. 46. 1880

Resources for Freedom: A Report to the President by The President's Materials Policy Commission, Volumes I and IV. 1952. Two volumes in one.

Schoolcraft, Henry R. **A View of the Lead Mines of Missouri.** 1819

Supplementary Report of the Land Planning Committee to the National Resources Board, 1935–1942

Thompson, John Giffin. **The Rise and Decline of the Wheat Growing Industry in Wisconsin** (Reprinted from *Bulletin of the University of Wisconsin,* No. 292). 1909

Timmons, John F. & William G. Murray, editors. **Land Problems and Policies.** 1950

U.S. Department of Agriculture—Forest Service. **Timber Resources for America's Future:** Forest Resource Report No. 14. 1958

U.S. Department of Agriculture—Soil Conservation Service and Forest Service. **Headwaters Control and Use.** 1937

U.S. Department of Commerce and Labor—Bureau of Corporations. **The Lumber Industry,** Parts I, II, & III. 1913/1914

U.S. Department of the Interior. **Hearings before the Secretary of the Interior on Leasing of Oil Lands.** 1906

Whitaker, J. Russell & Edward A. Ackerman. **American Resources:** Their Management and Conservation. 1951